A Taste of Torah

ב"ה

"How sweet are Your words to my taste…" Psalm 119:103

A Taste of Torah

A Devotional Study through the Five Books of Moses

Keren Hannah Pryor

Center for Judaic-Christian Studies
Dayton, Ohio

www.jcstudies.com

Published by the
Center for Judaic-Christian Studies
P.O. Box 750815
Dayton, OH 45475
U.S.A.

Tel: 937-434-4550
www.jcstudies.com

ISBN 0-918873-06-1

Printed in the United States of America.

Contents

Foreword by Dr. D.A. Pryor ix

Acknowledgments xiii

Introduction: xv

The Gift of Torah xv
The Universality of Torah xvi
"A Taste of Torah" xix

GENESIS – *B'reishit*

The Garden – Place of Intimacy 1

B'reishit – In the Beginning 3
Noach – Noah 8
Lekh Lekha – Go Ye! 12
Va'yera – And He Appeared 17
Chayei Sarah – Sarah's Life 22
Toldot – Generations 27
Va'yetze – And He Went Out 32
Va'yishlach – And He Sent 37
Va'yeishev – And He Dwelt 42
Miketz – At the End 46
Va'yigash – And Came Near 51
Va'yechi – And He Lived 55

EXODUS – *Shemot*

Exile – Place of Redemption 59

Shemot – Names 61
Va'era – And I Appeared 65
Bo – Come 69
Beshalach – When He Sent 73
Yitro – Jethro 77
Mishpatim – Judgments 83
Terumah – Heave Offering 88
Tetzaveh – You Shall Command 93
Ki Tissa – When You Take 99
Vayak'hel – And He Assembled 103
Pekudei – Accounts 107

LEVITICUS – *Vayikra*

The Tabernacle – Place of Connection 111

Vayikra – And He Called 113
Tzav – Command 118
Shemini – Eighth 122
Tazria – Conceived 127
Metzora – Leper 131
Acharei Mot –After the Death 134
Kedoshim – Holy 140
Emor – Say 144
Behar – On Mount Sinai 148
Bechukotai – In My Statutes 152

NUMBERS – *B'midbar*

The Wilderness – Place of Revelation 157

B'midbar – In the Wilderness 159
Nasso – Take a Census 164

Be'ha'alotekha – When You Set Up 169
Shlach Lekha – Send Thou 173
Korach – Korah 177
Chukkat – Statute 181
Balak – Balak 185
Pinchas – Phinehas 190
Mattot – Tribes 194
Massei – Journeys 198

DEUTERONOMY – *Devarim*

The Land – Place of Promise 202

Devarim – Words 204
Va'etchanan – And I Besought 208
Ekev – Because 213
Re'eh – Behold! 218
Shoftim – Judges 222
Ki Teitze – When You Go Out 227
Ki Tavo – When You Come 232
Nitzavim – You Are Standing 237
Va'yelekh – And He Went 243
Ha'azinu – Give Ear 247
Ve'zot ha'Brakha – And This is the Blessing 253

Appendix 1
Blessing Before the Study of Torah 257
Blessing After the Study of Torah 258

Appendix 2
Hebrew Pronunciation Guide 259

Bibliography 263

Foreword

by Dr. D. A. Pryor

One sermon you seldom hear in churches today is Jesus' great love for the Law. Yes, contrary to what you may have heard, Jesus entirely shared the sentiment of the Psalmist who wrote: *"Oh how I love Thy Law!"* (119:97).

Such a declaration may sound alien to the Christian ear, conditioned by centuries of theological traditions that speak of "the Law" mostly in negative terms. It is that which condemns us in our sins and from which Christ came to set us free. By "fulfilling" the Law (Matthew 5:17), it is said, Christ effectively brought it to an "end" (Romans 10:4). How can we speak then of Jesus' having great affection for "the Law"?

First we must go back, beyond twenty-first century Protestant, Catholic or Orthodox traditions, all the way to first-century Judaism. We must travel beyond Wittenberg, Rome and Constantinople to Jerusalem and the Land of Israel. There we will find a devout first-century Jewish rabbi from Nazareth named *Yeshua* (Jesus), for whom the *Torah* (Law) was "God-breathed" scripture and life-affirming instruction from a gracious Father.

To get a better sense of his different worldview, try substituting "Word" for "Law" when you read the Hebrew Bible. *"Oh how I love Thy Word!"* flows as naturally even from our lips as the Psalmist's version would have from Jesus'. In fact the terms "Word" (*Davar*) and "Law" (*Torah*) often are used in parallel in Scripture. For instance:

And many people shall go and say, Come ye, and let us go up to the mountain of the Lord, *to the house of the God of Jacob;*

and he will teach us of his ways, and we will walk in his paths: for out of Zion shall go forth the ***Law*** *[Torah] and the* ***Word*** *[Davar] of the* L*ORD* *from Jerusalem. (Isaiah 2:3 KJV)*

Second, recognize that the English word "law" (from the Greek *nomos*) connotes something less than heart-warming for most of us, unlike the Hebrew word *Torah* which has a positive ring to the Jewish ear. The Torah is that which is "perfect and restores the soul" (Psalm 19:7), engenders "delight" and is worthy of focused meditation "day and night" (Psalm 1:2). It was that which Jesus memorized and studied as a child, interpreted for his disciples and commended them for observing, expounded upon in his Sermon on the Mount, and continually in his life and teaching 'filled-full' of the Father's intended meaning. Oh how he loved the Torah!

Finally, here are four foundational Hebraic principles that will help you develop Jesus' positive attitude toward the Torah (Law) and prepare you for the appetizing fare that awaits you in *A Taste of Torah.*

> 1] The Torah is a loving Father's ***teaching***. The Hebrew word *torah* fundamentally connotes guidance and instruction—that which aims you so that you hit the mark. And the mark for the Torah always is life. Much more than "the Law," it is God's will, wisdom and direction conveyed in love to His covenant children for their ongoing fellowship with the Holy One of Israel.
>
> 2] The Torah is a ***treasure***. Only in light of the above can we appreciate the Psalmist's attitude: "O how I love your Torah!" Psalm 119 consists of 8 verses for each of the 22 letters of the Hebrew alphabet, and every one of the 176 verses extols an aspect of the multi-faceted Torah.
>
> 3] The Torah is a ***gift of the Spirit***. The Torah was written by the "finger of God" (Exodus 31:18; Deuteronomy 9:10). This Hebrew idiom is found in Luke 11:20 and explained

in the parallel of Matthew 12:28. It means "the Spirit of God." Truly the Torah—the foundational "Scripture" to which the Apostle Paul alludes in 2 Timothy 3:16—is "inspired". Said another way, it is "in-Spirited".

4] The Torah is ***guidance for a redeemed people.*** The Law was given to Israel *after* they had been saved out of Egypt, not as the basis or means of their salvation. It was meant to guide the covenant people in paths of righteousness that would bring them to their appointed place of promise and productivity. It is good to remember in this regard that these things "were written for our instruction" as well (1 Corinthians 10:11).

In Jesus' first-century world, the Torah was read every Sabbath in the synagogue (cf. Acts 15:21), even as it is today. It is at the heart of Jewish worship. The selection, called the *parasha* or portion, is accompanied by a "concluding" or *haftarah* reading from the Prophets. For example, Jesus read the *haftarah* from the Book of Isaiah at the synagogue in Nazareth.

A Taste of Torah gives you commentary on all fifty-four portions. (A schedule of the annual readings for each Shabbat and the biblical festivals can be found on the website, www.jcstudies.com.) Keren Hannah also references a reading portion from the *Brit Chadasha* (New Testament) that connects in meaning with the *parasha* and *haftarah.*

Today, Christians are twenty centuries and two cultures removed from the Jewish world and Hebraic perspective that were so essential to the life and teachings of Yeshua and that informed the authors of the New Testament. The good news however is that in our time the true and living God is restoring the State of Israel, and with it, realigning the Church on its Jerusalem foundations, firmly rooting it in the fertile soil of Second Temple Judaism from which it sprang. The followers of Jesus of Nazareth are being reconnected to the nourishing sap of the olive tree of Abraham, Isaac and Jacob, and spiritually enriched by a Jewish inheritance.

Among the servants the Lord is raising up to communicate this precious Hebraic heritage is Keren Hannah Pryor. In her heart is a highway to Zion that God sovereignly implanted. Having lived in the Land for much of her life and speaking Hebrew, Keren has inherited the Jewish mindset of our Lord. Diligently she has studied the Hebrew Bible with a devotion kindled by the fire of the Holy Spirit and a deep love for its Author.

In her writing Keren gives you a taste of what she has savored for many years, the sweetness of God's Word and the inspired instruction of His Torah. She gleans from the wisdom of Jewish sages and commentators as well as Christian insights into the *Tanakh* (Old Testament), and conveys them in a gentle but profound manner that will inspire and inform every student of Scripture.

A Taste of Torah will give you precious Hebraic glimpses into the grace and beauty of the Holy Scriptures that were revered by Jesus, Paul, the Apostles and the First Church. It is a book that sanctifies the name of the God of Israel, even as its author lives up to her own Hebrew name, *Keren Hannah,* "gracious ray of light." A feast awaits you, dear reader. Taste and see! It's good!

Dr. Dwight A. Pryor
Jerusalem, Israel
Dayton, Ohio

Acknowledgments

Albeit in connection with a humble endeavor such as this, I am overwhelmed at the generosity, encouragement and painstaking effort of those who have under-girded me through it all. It is with a glad and grateful heart that I take this opportunity to acknowledge these shining souls.

All of you, the *"A Taste of Torah" students*—those I have the pleasure of knowing personally and those I have never met. Thanks to your devotion and love of the eternal Word of God, I have been inspired to seek His face and to learn far more than I would have otherwise.

The staff at the Center, my dear fellow travelers: *James Whitman*, *Joyce Ransdell*, and *Eileen Sullivan*. You have been an inspiration and have greatly encouraged me along the way.

Cindy Elliot, a faithful servant of *Adonai*, who has managed the e-mail study lists for me. Words cannot express my appreciation of your generous spirit and sweet and constant encouragement.

Our dear friends *John and Lucy Talbot*, and *Dolly MacDonald*. Your loving-kindness and *tzedakah* have been an enormous help in sustaining a home-base in Jerusalem during the many months of Dwight's and my commitment to our various teaching and writing projects.

The Zakaims! Zion and Irit, Alon and Eli—a special part of our Jerusalem 'family'! *Rav todot* for your strong friendship, care, and the many delicious meals that strengthened us in our work. *Barukh HaShem*!

Dov Chaiken, Jerusalem friend and Hebrew mentor, who edited the Hebrew content of the manuscript with his keen insight and graciously offered significant advice. Any discrepancies in this area are totally mine.

Rivkah Levy and her husband *Laiv*, of Drawing Board Studios, who gave shape and form to this book. Their devoted servants' hearts and extraordinary expertise and patience are very deeply appreciated.

Kelly DeBaar, graphic designer, whose creative skills and efforts are valued, and her friendly, giving heart more so.

Jane Richards, who together with her husband *Peter*, are loving, enduring, and constantly encouraging friends to Dwight and me. Jane, you were the obedient instrument used of the Lord that prompted me to start the e-mail series. Thank you.

Last but not least, my beloved husband *Dwight A. Pryor*, who shared his invaluable editorial insights of the original e-mail series of 'A Taste of Torah' and who has borne patiently with my absorption in this project. Our union is God's greatest gift to me.

To all mentioned above, and to the many I have failed to mention of whom I ask forgiveness, I extend my heartfelt thanks. May the God of Israel and Yeshua, the Living Word and the Light of the World, always illumine your path and make joyous your journey.

And finally, *acharon ha-acharon chaviv*, to whom I am grateful beyond words, the One who is the reason and source of all life and all light, our eternal Father and King. To Him be all glory, now and forever. Amen.

Introduction

The Gift of Torah

God presented His Word to His people as a light and a path. If we choose to walk in His path, in the illumination of His light, we find that we are enabled to live the life He gave us in the most fulfilled and rewarding manner possible.

We become aware, soon after setting out, that this walk is primarily a means of growing in loving, covenant relationship with our Father God. Enfolded in this relationship, we grow in ever-increasing intimate knowledge of Him. All of God's Word, we discover to our wonder, is a gift of life in that it is a gracious revelation of Himself the Source of Life.

At Mount Sinai, the God of Abraham, Isaac, and Jacob made a powerful first appearance to His newly redeemed people, the family of Israel. There He gave them His teaching and guidance—recorded in written form on tablets of stone by the "finger of God", the Holy Spirit (Ex. 31:18; Deut. 9:10; Luke 11:20), and then extended on scrolls of parchment by Moses. These became known as the Torah, the first five books of the Bible. It is our privilege and joy to study the timeless truth contained in this foundation upon which stands all consequent revelation of God. It is the rock, as it were, upon which the House of God is built on earth.

This book is primarily designed to accompany the study of the Bible on a weekly basis, working within the framework of the *Parshiyot haShavua* (the designated weekly portions of the Annual Reading Cycle that are read in synagogues on Shabbat). I believe the student of the Word will find it helpful as an additional tool, while keeping the primary focus on the biblical text.

The regular study of Torah, as with all worthwhile endeavors, requires commitment and effort. However, if we approach this "Rock," not impersonally and analytically as a geologist, but with our hearts open to respond, with ears eager to hear and eyes searching for wonder, we will discover that it too contains a heart and offers life beyond our greatest expectations. From the heart of this Rock flows a stream of living water that refreshes the weary, strengthens the weak, and brings healing and wholeness to the soul. It brings life where there is none and causes *the desert to bloom…abundantly and to rejoice with joy and singing* (Isaiah 35:1-2).

The Universality of Torah

The command was given to the children of Israel, the descendants of the beloved patriarchs Abraham, Isaac and Jacob, that they were to teach the Torah to their children in order that all future generations would come to know the One true God.

> *He established a testimony in Jacob and appointed a law in Israel, which he commanded our fathers to teach to their children, that the next generation might know them, the children yet unborn, and arise and tell them to their children…* (Psalm 78:5-6).

The universality of God as Creator and King of all the earth is proclaimed in the Scriptures, for example:

> *The earth is the LORD's and th e fullness thereof, the world and those who dwell therein…* (Psalm 24:1).
>
> *There is none like you, O* Lord; *you are great, and your name is great in might. Who would not fear you, O King of the nations?* (Jeremiah 10:6-7).

> *And they sing the song of Moses, the servant of God, and the song of the Lamb, saying, "Great and amazing are your deeds, O Lord God the Almighty! Just and true are your ways, O King of the nations!"* (Revelation 15:3).

Jewish literature and the commentaries of the Sages carry the understanding that God's revelation of Himself and the gift of His Torah are meant for all peoples of the earth—all God's children who are created in His image.

The renowned Rabbi S.R. Hirsch (Germany, 1808-1888) writes in the introduction to his excellent commentary on the Psalms:

> At the very beginning, Abraham was appointed to be "the spiritual father of the multitude of the nations." It was through him, and through the generations that would follow him, that blessings were to come "to all the families of the earth."

Hirsch presents thought provoking insights on Psalm 47, which exalts the Lord who loves all peoples and who is *a great King over all the earth*. He comments on verses 8-9:

> God reigns over the nations; God sits on his holy throne. The princes of the peoples gather as the people of the God of Abraham

> [The Lord] chose for His very own Abraham and the nation that was to descend from him. By this act, the Lord created an instrument that was to light the way for mankind in its wanderings through time and to ensure man's eventual return to God, and his attainment of that salvation that can be won on earth only through God.

God came down in further revelation of Himself "*in the fullness of time*" (Ephesians 1:10) when His Word of Life was enfleshed in *Yeshua haMashiach*—Jesus the Anointed One—of whom the Father proclaimed: "*This is My beloved Son, with whom I am well pleased; listen to Him*" (Matthew 17:5; Mark 9:7).

Yeshua taught and lived and demonstrated the will of His Father. The Light of the Word shone as a beacon of hope to those who were who were far from God and without hope in the world.

> *"I have come into the world as light, so that whoever believes in me may not remain in darkness"* (John12:46).

In Him the knowledge of the God of Israel would go forth to the ends of the earth so that *"whosoever... is thirsty may come and take the water of life freely"* (Revelation 22:17). As Yeshua proclaimed at the height of the joyous, light-filled, water pouring ceremony during the Feast of Tabernacles in Jerusalem:

> *"... but whosoever drinks of the water that I shall give him shall never thirst; but the water that I shall give him shall become in him a well of water springing up unto eternal life"* (John 4:14).

In Him the transcendent purposes of God come together in perfect unity. The water-giving Rock that accompanied the Israelites through the wilderness found its resting place as the foundation stone in the Holy of Holies in Jerusalem. Incarnate, it became the cornerstone of the living Temple being built as the dwelling place of God in the earth. It will again be established in the City of God on Mount Zion when a river of life-giving waters, as described in the prophet Ezekiel's vision (Ez.47), will flow forth from the throne of the King of kings.

> *"And he showed me a river of water of life, bright as crystal, proceeding out of the throne of God and of the Lamb, in the midst of the street thereof. And on this side of the river and on that was the tree of life... and the leaves of the tree were for the healing of the nations"* (Revelation 22:1-2).

"A Taste of Torah"

On my personal journey from Mount Sinai to Mount Zion and beyond, which is a continuous cycle between the two that spirals ever upwards, I have a huge debt of gratitude to the many "hewers of the Rock" whose lives have been devoted to the study and sharing of God's Word. The rich insights and commentaries of Torah scholars and the Sages of past generations, as well as the present, and the varied input of scholars and students of the *Brit Chadasha* (the New Testament or, literally, the Renewed Covenant) have greatly enriched my life and understanding of the God of Israel and His Word.

This rendition of "*A Taste of Torah*" is offered humbly as a miniscule sampling of the amazingly rich and lavish banquet of Torah thought and commentary that exists. It reflects some of the riches I have received through my personal study of the Scriptures and the teaching and commentaries that have inspired and informed me, particularly during the past twenty years of regular weekly 'encounters' with the *parasha* (prescribed Torah portion).

The weekly study of "*A Taste of Torah*" that has been sent out via e-mail from the Center for Judaic-Christian Studies since February 2005, was drawn in part from the notes I have collected over the years from a wide variety of sources. The sources are quoted wherever possible and a bibliography is listed. I sincerely ask forgiveness for any source that has been forgotten or overlooked.

There are many references to the Hebrew text in these studies. The eternal truths of God are embedded in the letters, words and syntax of the Hebrew Scriptures. Every small word is a treasure-store of meaning. Through my own study and love of Hebrew, I have arrived at an understanding of the truth that Hebrew is more than "just another language". It is a unique means of gaining deeper understanding of God's Word. It is after all the ancient tongue that our Father in Heaven chose as the means of communicating with His children. It has now been resurrected to vibrant life as a significant element of His present restoration of Israel. His unchanging Word to us is written in a language that has remained constant through the centuries. Hebrew has proved to be enduring as well as beautiful. If you are unfamiliar with the language, I trust that you will enjoy the discovery of it.

May you continue to delight in the Rock of our Salvation as you drink of the living waters and enjoy the sweet and nourishing honey contained and expressed in His Word.

Eat, my friends. Drink, yes drink abundantly, O beloved!
(Song of Songs 5:1).

Keren Hannah

Jerusalem, Israel (Hanukkah 5768, December 2007)
Dayton, Ohio, USA, 2008

GENESIS

B'reishit - בְּרֵאשִׁית

The Garden - Place of Intimacy

We read in this first book of Torah of the beginning of all created matter: God spoke and it was done. The Creator, with His breath and His Word, brought light, substance and life from darkness and chaos. He created the universe from a void of nothingness. A void He Himself formed, we can surmise, by the partial contraction of His Presence, which fills all in all.

This vast mystery of Creation is presented as a relatively brief account in the Scriptures. More text will be devoted to the first recorded marriage—that of *Yitzchak* and *Rivkah* (Isaac and Rebekah)—than to the whole Creation account. This indicates, perhaps, that what we can learn from the subject of marriage is more significant, and affords more practical application for our journey through life, than gaining deeper knowledge of how the earth was created.

The Garden of Eden, with its vibrant and peaceful beauty, was the initial setting created by God for His beloved children. It was an environment wherein true relationship and intimacy could grow and flourish, and be enjoyed with pure delight.

Here, at the beginning, let us prepare our hearts to study the *parasha* each week as an exploration of the Living Word. Each *parasha* is a God-inspired portion of narrative that continues to speak to our lives today just as it has to the lives of children of God throughout the centuries. As we set our hearts to search out the treasures the Author has stored for our discovery, let us not insist on reaching final conclusions. May we be more concerned with discovering His truth than with proving theories. Let us set aside any rigid, preconceived notions and take delight in wrestling with the relationships, patterns, and symbols described; be enamored with the wonder of the Word itself.

As we approach the text with open ears, eyes and hearts we can trust that we will hear the gracious whisper of the Spirit of God and see what the "finger of God" is pointing out to us. He is faithful to *lead us into all truth* (John 16:3).

To quote Avivah Zornberg, an outstanding teacher of Torah, who has enriched my personal study through those of her weekly teachings I have been privileged to attend in Jerusalem and via her creative books of commentary on Genesis and Exodus:

> Life is strange territory, it requires the compass, the orientation of biblical guidance. The Bible is familiar, life is strange. We bring the two together to shed light on life.

B'reishit - בראשית

In the Beginning

Genesis 1:1–6:8; Isaiah 42:5–43:10;
Revelation 19:6–16; 21:1–7

B'reishit bara Elohim et ha'shamayim ve'et ha'aretz.

In the beginning God created the heavens and the earth.
(Genesis 1:1)

The first verse of the Torah consists of seven Hebrew words, corresponding to the seven days of Creation. The life of all things flows from and is suspended upon these seven words. They tell us that this universe has a Creator. They clearly proclaim that it is not an arbitrary accident but came into existence by intentional design.

The inherent purpose and meaning of this existence, as well as the character and reality of the Creator, are mysteries for man to discover. The choice to attempt to discern these mysteries is ours. We are not left wandering in the dark, however, for God chose to weave revelation of Himself into the Creation itself. As the Psalmist, David, sings:

> *The heavens declare the glory of God, and the sky above proclaims his handiwork. Day to day pours out speech [words], and night to night reveals knowledge* (19:1-2).

Rabbi S.R. Hirsch paraphrases verse 2 of the Psalm beautifully:

> One day speaks to the other, "Rise up and serve the Word," and one night says to the other, "Lie down in peace, there is one 'Knowledge' [all-knowing One] that watches over you." [1]

God created man and woman in His image (1:26). That mark of Himself within us causes our hearts to leap in recognition when we encounter Him in some way. It resonates deeply within us when we see a reflection of His beauty revealed in the wonders of nature, of His Word, of one another. Whenever we recognize Him our response can only be joyous, awe-filled worship.

The Power of Words

This first book of the Bible relates the origins of the world, the history of humanity and the formation of the people of Israel. The central purpose of all Creation, as we see indicated in the Garden of Eden, is the intimate relationship between God and mankind. God spoke all things into being. When God created man He endowed him with the gift of speech; an essential ability that naturally set him apart from the animals. It follows that the primary, creative means of forging relationship is the ability to communicate with words.

The Sages of Israel maintain that not only does each word of the written Torah contain great depth and significance but the individual letters, and even the spaces around the letters and words, have intrinsic meaning. Indeed, right here at the beginning, the first Hebrew letter of the Torah is a *bet* and the space around it forms a large, invisible letter *peh*. *Peh* is also the Hebrew word for mouth. Thus we see a visual illustration of the fact that all of Scripture proceeds from the mouth of the invisible God, Who spoke all things into being.

God, our Father, desires relationship with the 'children' He creates, and He places within them the core need and desire for relationship with Himself and with one another. Our words contain the power to satisy this need to create intimacy and unity and to facilitate meeting and fellowship—both with God and with one another.

The First Marriage

All else in creation was spoken into existence but the first human being was formed by the hands of God. *He formed* (*vayitzer*—literally, shaped or molded) *man from the dust of the earth* (2:7). Then God breathed the animating life of His spirit into man's form. This is a powerful indication of the loving, personal involvement of God in His creation of man. It is also a witness to the creative blessing inherent in the loving touch of a father's hand upon his children.

The first human was a single being—Adam. The primary task God assigns him is to name the animals. When he sees that the animals are in pairs, each with his mate, he becomes aware of his alone-ness. We may assume that God intended him to recognize his solitary existence and experience the yearning for an "other". In response God says: "*It is not good for man to be alone; I will make a fitting helper for him*" (2:18). Here begins the earthly expression of love, of life in relationship; the *inter*-dependence that is the antidote for solitary independence and selfishness. The possibility is created for the formation of a relationship one to another that opens and expands the human heart. In embracing the "other" our capacity is similarly extended to embrace our Father-God in a growing, ever more intimate relationship.

God, again with His own hands, separates Eve from Adam and brings the two together in the beauty of the Garden. God is the Matchmaker and officiates, as it were, the first marriage.

Humanity's dance of love begins, the culmination of which will be another glorious marriage. The union is expressed at Sinai with the betrothal between God and His people Israel and reaches radiant, joyful conclusion at the wedding banquet of the Lamb and His Bride. A conclusion, like every wedding, that is a new beginning!

The First Murder

> You take paradise and put up a parking lot.
>
> —Joni Mitchell

We learn from the beginning of Torah, in the unfolding drama of Adam and Eve's sin and expulsion from the Garden, that true sanctity is linked to obedience to the will of God. As Shlomo Riskin, a renowned rabbi in Israel, points out,

> The Torah insists that the division between good and evil, or right and wrong cannot be left to the whim of an individual. Good is what God says is good, evil is what God says is evil.[2]

The seductive message of the Snake, then and throughout history is the very antithesis of this concept: "Did God really say?" Or even more prevalent today, "Who cares what God says?"

Riskin also notes Sigmund Freud's conclusion that, left to his own devices, every human is a genius in the art of self-justification[3]. We instinctively find ways to rationalize and justify what we decide we want to do. Once we throw off the anchor of stability and direction of God's will and Word, we find ourselves in a chaotic world of unlimited choice, confusing possibilities and unrelenting temptation. In further revelation this Word of God … *became flesh and dwelt among us full of grace and truth* (John 1:14). It became the Living Word, in physicality, in the Messiah *Yeshua* (Jesus).

A consequence of Adam and Eve's rebellion and fall is the first murder. Sin always leads to death in some form. The narrative relates that God accepts the sacrifice offered by Abel and rejects Cain's. Instead of humbly learning from the experience as to what pleases God, Cain is filled with jealousy and anger towards his brother. As a caring parent, God gently cautions Cain to repent of his attitude and warns, "*If you do not do well, sin crouches at your doorstep. Its desire is for you, but you must rule over it*" (4:4-5). How sweet Cain's repentance could have been, and what joy he would have brought to the Father's heart through his willing obedience. Cain would not hear, however, and he proceeds to spill the blood of his brother.

We all have freedom of choice to hear, repent and to obey God's voice. As those redeemed by the grace of God, we are able to lift our downcast faces and receive the strength to overcome the sin that continually crouches at the threshold of our lives and aims for our destruction. God has *provided Himself the lamb* (Genesis 22:8) and we are delivered and cleansed of this consequence of the first Adam's sin by the blood of the last Adam, Yeshua. In the ultimate sacrifice of obedience, He provided atonement for the sin of mankind and defeated death. In Him the way is made open for all to return to the Garden and to enjoy sweet fellowship with our Father God, the Source of all life.

---

[1] Rabbi Samson Raphael Hirsch (Germany, 1808-1888); *The Hirsch Psalms*, 136.

[2] Rabbi Shlomo Riskin (Efrat, Israel), *Torah Lights, Genesis Confronts Life, Love and Family*, 46.

[4] Ibid., 47.

Noach - נח

Noah

Genesis 6:9–11:32; Isaiah 54:1–55:5;
Matthew 24:36–44

A Tale of Two Generations

This powerful *parasha* begins and ends with two major disasters inflicted upon mankind as a consequence of sin. The first, in the time of Noah, was the flood. This disaster destroyed the world's population, apart from those who found sanctuary in the Ark. The sin of this generation is obvious—rampant immorality, corruption, greed and envy. Man lusted after his own fleeting pursuits and had no regard for the glory or purposes of God.

The disaster at the conclusion of the parasha is the fall of the Tower of Babel, when the unity and common language of mankind is destroyed. The evil evidenced in this generation is more subtle. The threat to the moral fiber and to the future of man lay in the attitude of the builders: "*Let us make a name for ourselves*" (11:4).

A vital lesson for us in this account is the understanding that while unity and community are biblical ideals blessed by God, they do carry an inherent danger. A community may come to regard itself as the purpose of its own existence and the value of both God and the individual become subordinated to it. This danger can be applied to any form of community, including the family, organizations, and religious congregations. If the community does not encourage individual members primarily to serve God rather than the group itself then the moral law of God, and ultimately God Himself, will be dispensed with. We see examples of this in Communist and other forms of dictatorship as well as in Western materialistic, humanistic democracies.

A religious community that may proclaim faith in God but compels members to submit to its commands and even to sacrifice their lives for its own power and glory becomes a god unto itself. In reality, these entities, in the spirit of the builders of the Tower of Babel, are building their own kingdom and not the Kingdom of the one true God.

Build an Ark

Noah was deemed righteous in his generation because he heard and obeyed God's voice. God commanded Noah to build an ark. The Hebrew word for ark is *tevah,* which also carries the meaning of 'letter' (of the Hebrew *aleph-bet*), and by extension 'word', which is built with letters. Noah and his family, as well as the animals, were saved as a result of obeying the word of God and entering the *Tevah*-Ark. By application, our hope of salvation in the flood of our present generation's iniquity is to hear and live in obedience to the Word and will of God; to find shelter in the place where God's Kingship and Kingdom rule is established—in Yeshua, the Living *Tevah*-Word.

The Baal Shem Tov (1700-1760), founder of the Hassidic movement in Eastern Europe, demonstrates how the physical measurements of Noah's Ark reflect the essence of language. The measurements are 300 cubits long, 50 cubits wide and 30 cubits high (Genesis 6:15). Each Hebrew letter has a numerical value. 300 is represented by *shin,* 50 by *nun* and 30 by *lamed.*

The three letters can be arranged to spell the word *lashon*, which means tongue, speech, and language.

We know that the ability to communicate, to share words with one another, is a major definition of our humanity. As well as life itself, God's greatest gift to us is revelation of Himself through His Word. This is highlighted by another *tevah*. Moses, the servant whom God chose to present the gift of the Torah to His people, was saved as a baby in an ark, a *tevah*. The ark of bulrushes, made by his mother and sister Miriam, wherein they placed him and then set him afloat on the Nile, was the means of his salvation. As a man Moses would transmit the Torah—God's guidance and direction towards the ultimate salvation, peace and redemption of the world. According to God's instructions, the symbol of this Word, the original stone tablets, were then placed in an ark of wood covered with gold—the Ark of the Covenant. God's dwelling place on the earth, first the Tabernacle and then the Temple, were centered upon this Ark containing the Word.

One God, One Language

This understanding of Ark-Word immediately highlights a connection between the Flood and the Tower of Babel. At that time of history, *The entire earth had one language, a common vocabulary* (11:1). However, instead of communicating with one another in love, the Midrash describes how in the building of the Tower[1]:

> If a stone fell to the ground and shattered, everyone groaned; if a human being fell to the ground and died, no one took notice.

The people had become materialistic and callous and were uncaring regarding the value and the needs of another. In response God caused them to speak multiple languages and they were scattered in confusion to all parts of the earth.

A principle in the interpretation of Scripture is "first mention"—taking note of the first time a key word or concept is introduced as it holds special significance. The verb *va'yered* (and he came down) appears for the first time in this parasha (11:5). God Himself comes down to see the city and tower the people are building. We understand that God is personally interested in the affairs of mankind and His desire is to dwell among them on the earth. This prepares us for future occasions when God will "come down". Rabbi S.R. Hirsch, in *The Pentateuch* his excellent commentary on the Torah, notes:

> The verb *va'yered* when used in connection with God always designates a crisis in the development of world affairs during which God's intervention...brings the world one step closer to its goal—the day when the *Shekinah* will be able to dwell once more among men on earth.

To accomplish His ultimate goal, God makes a humble, seemingly insignificant beginning. From all the families on earth He chooses a man, *Avraham*, who will carry this message and teach it to his family and to all who will hear. Then He "comes down" and reveals Himself to this people at Sinai and they become the nation Israel; through whom He will once again "come down" Himself as a tiny baby, the Anointed One—Yeshua the Messiah—to further the redemption of the world. In the fullness of time, He will ultimately come down as King and Judge of all the nations, at which time He promises:

> *Then will I return to the people a pure language that they may all call upon the name of the* Lord, *to serve Him with one accord* (Zephanaiah 3:9).

Then His Name will be One and we will all worship Him with one holy tongue. *Halleluyah!*

---

[1] Misrash is the vast collection of rabbinic homiletic literature and imaginative commentary on the Torah.

Lekh Lekha - לך לך

Go Forth

Genesis 12:1–17:27; Isaiah 40:27–41:16;
Romans 3:19–4:3

There were ten generations from Adam to Noah, and now, ten generations after Noah, we are introduced to an even greater character in the Biblical narrative: Abram, who will be renamed Abraham. Why does God choose Abram? We are not explicitly told. We are informed, however, that God chose him to be the father of His family on earth. God promises to make his name great and to bless him. More than that, He makes the following greatly expanded promise: "*And I will bless them that bless thee, and him that curses thee I will curse, and in thee shall all the nations of the earth be blessed* (12:3).

A hint as to the character of Abram is given in his immediate, unquestioning response to God's command to leave his land and father's house and to go forth "*to the land that I will show you*" (12:1). The prophet Nehemiah reveals an important insight regarding Abraham: *Finding his heart true to You, You made a covenant with him* (9:7-8). This "true heart," filled with faithfulness and loyalty towards God, is demonstrated time and time again throughout Abraham's life.

Covenant requires true hearts. Only on the basis of loyalty and trust can true covenant be entered into. We read in the parasha that, after reassuring Abraham with the beautiful promise, *Fear not Abram, I am a shield to you; your reward shall be very great* (15:1), God establishes an eternal covenant with him. As confirmation of the covenant a *heh*, the letter of breath of the Divine Name—YHWH (*yod, heh, vav, heh*), is added to his and to his wife's names. Abram becomes Abraham (Compassionate father) and Sarai becomes Sarah (Princess).

A change of name, biblically, is of great significance and symbolizes a transformation of character and destiny. It indicates, as it were, a new life, a new birth. God also commands that the act of circumcision, which Abraham is to perform on himself and his descendants after him, is to be the physical, outward sign of this covenant (17:9-14). The promises of God, that Abraham would be the father of many nations (17:4) and that his offspring would inhabit the Land of Canaan forever (17:8), are confirmed by the covenant.

Go to Yourself!

The title of each *parasha* is taken from key words in the first sentence that contain the essence or central theme of the portion and even of the Torah itself. The two Hebrew words of this week's title, *lekh lekha* (literally 'Go ye'), can also be translated, "Go to yourself." The renowned medieval commentator Rashi (France, 1049-1105) comments:

> *The Lord was saying, "You will gain from the journey. '**Lekha**,' to yourself, will be the benefit."*

The call to go is difficult. It's a challenge to cut yourself off from your environment and from all that is familiar. This is especially difficult when, as with Abraham, it is a venture into the unknown. Adam and Eve were sent out from the Garden in shame, and Cain was commanded to wander the earth as a curse, but God assures Abraham that in his case his going forth would be for blessing.

His calling is similar to that of every new bride and groom who must leave their "father's house" and cleave to their beloved spouse. They, too, embark upon a journey of adventure into the unknown. With true hearts they become united in the creative process of discovering and blessing the other and find, as a result, that the blessing and the benefits therefrom rebound to themselves. Abraham too, in his going, would be completed and perfected, and in fact would become a "new creation."

A Goodly Fragrance

> *But thanks be to God, who in Messiah always leads us in triumph, and through us spreads the fragrance of the knowledge of him everywhere* (2 Corinthians 2:14).

In the Talmud (Bereishit Rabah 39,2) Rav Berekiah said:

> Avraham resembled a phial of myrrh tightly closed and lying in a corner, so that its fragrance was not disseminated; as soon as it was taken up [and moved about] its fragrance was disseminated.

In his pagan homeland Abram had come to know the one true God and was filled with the fragrance of the knowledge of Him. It was only when God stirred Abraham and moved him from place to place that this fragrance was shed abroad and was able to stir others.

> *Thine ointments have a goodly fragrance; thy name is as ointment poured forth* (Song of Songs 1:3).

The purpose of fragrance is to attract, to inspire, to beautify. Abraham, to an even greater measure than our forefathers Isaac and Jacob, was filled with the beauty of truth, wisdom and loving-kindness. His nature was to reach out, to connect lovingly and joyfully with his fellow man in faithful, loving, obedient service to God, evidenced in his constant deeds of righteousness. Thus, as Abraham exalted God's Name through his obedient service and wholehearted worship, God caused Abraham's name to be made great in the earth. In addition the fragrance of his being was spilled out to inspire all future generations.

El Shaddai

El Shaddai means the One who nurtures and provides life-giving sustenance, in the manner of a nursing mother. God introduces Himself to Abraham by this name before He presents the following challenge to him: *Walk in My ways and be blameless [perfect]* (17:1). Abraham's understandable response is to throw himself on his face!

The *Etz Hayim* (Tree of Life) commentary adds that the Midrash offers an understanding of *El Shaddai* as: The God who says 'Enough!' (Hebrew: *Dai!*). It's as if God is saying:

> The people of the world have gone on long enough acting like children. It is time to demand righteous behavior of them, to proclaim that certain things are permitted and others forbidden.

Abraham no doubt was overwhelmed by the commission to teach humanity the meaning of a God-centered life. He realized the responsibility entailed in his calling to be the example and teacher of the ways of the holy God. This is a challenge we all are given as Abraham's children, the family of God, the household of faith. It is one echoed by Yeshua Himself: "*Follow [walk after] Me!*[2]" He came to embody the teaching of God and to demonstrate the way in which we are exhorted to walk—the same path Abraham saw stretching before him when God said, "*Lekh, lekha*!"

Yeshua said, "*Abraham saw My day and was glad.*[3]" Prophetically Abraham saw God's provision of His own beloved

Son to light the way, and his heart rejoiced. May we be encouraged to keep walking after Him, in His perfect way of the Spirit—constantly moving, learning and growing, and rejoicing in the hope set before us. In so doing may we too spread the fragrance of the knowledge of God wherever He leads us.

---

[1] Tanchuma 25, Solomon Buber edition.

[2] Luke 9:23

[3] John 8:56

Va'yera - וירא

And Appeared

Genesis 18:1–22:24; 2 Kings 4:1–37; James 2:14–24

The first words of the *parasha* are profound and startling: *And God appeared to him.* They vibrate in remarkable contrast to the simple, every-day remainder of the sentence: … *beneath the trees of Mamre, as he was sitting before the door of his tent in the heat of the day* (18:1). This seems to indicate that God's Presence is indeed everywhere. He appears in normal, routine settings but unless we are watching with intention, as Abraham was, we will not be aware of it.

There appears to be a connection with the timing of the revelation and the circumstances of Abraham's life. In obedience to God's command, Abraham recently had performed the first act of *brit milah* (covenant of circumcision) on himself and the males of his household. This was to be the symbolic physical sign of God's covenant with him and his future descendants—a constant reminder that the body and its inclinations are to be subjected to the will of the Lord and to His true and loving ways.

A Dramatic Visual Aid

What is the purpose of this appearance of God, the Lord, to our forefather Abraham? He discloses to Abraham the imminent destruction of the two most affluent and self-indulgent cities in the land—the very land God promised to Abraham's descendants according to the covenant. Sodom and Gomorrah represent everything that is in opposition to the ways of God. The outpouring of His judgment upon the wickedness of these cities and their total destruction would be a vivid and dramatic visual aid and a warning to the future people of God. By teaching his children well, Abraham must ensure they are thoroughly grounded in the way of truth—the way God is teaching Abraham—and that they in turn will teach their children throughout the generations. Only in this way will the selfish, sinful characteristics of Sodom and Gomorrah not take root among the children of Abraham when they eventually inherit and prosper in the God-given *"good and spacious land"* (Deuteronomy 8:7-14).

In effect, the covenant set Abraham apart as holy to God. He was separated in a real way from the world around him that was idolatrous, decadent and filled with wickedness. Abraham's life and spirit of service to God and his love of mankind stand in stark juxtaposition to the surrounding world, exemplified by Sodom. For example, as illustrated in the parasha, Abraham's tent was always open to strangers, whom he respectfully welcomed and was quick to serve. Sodom, on the other hand, was hostile to strangers. Hospitality and begging were forbidden by law. The city bred hatred, violence and widespread immorality. The way of God that Abraham epitomized, on the other hand, was one of brotherly love and kindness, of giving to those in need, and was characterized by purity and modesty.

Set Apart but not Isolated

A valuable lesson we can learn from Abraham is that to be "holy and set apart" to our God does not mean to be isolated from humanity. Abraham remained actively involved in the circumstances around him. This is highlighted by his almost audacious intercession for the swaying of God's judgment on Sodom and Gomorrah. It is lived out in his zeal to find every opportunity to eagerly serve his fellow man. It is worth noting, however, that Abraham did not *move his tent toward Sodom* as Lot did (13:12). He did not place himself and his household in the midst of evil, in the way of temptation. He trusted God to lead him as to where to pitch his tent and then he faithfully and lovingly served those God brought his way. His life is echoed in the words of poet Sam Walter Foss[1]:

> Why should I sit in the scorner's seat
> or hurl the cynic's ban?
> Let me live in my house by the side of the road
> And be a friend to man.

As "new creations" in Yeshua we are holy and set apart unto God; we are called, like Abraham, to walk by the Spirit in the ways of the Lord:

> *... in order that the righteous requirement of the Torah might be fulfilled in us, who walk not according to the flesh but according to the Spirit. For those who live according to the flesh set their minds on the things of the flesh, but those who live according to the Spirit set their minds on the things of the Spirit. To set the mind on the flesh is death, but to set the mind on the Spirit is life and peace*" (Romans 8:4-6).

This does not mean that we draw apart from the world as isolated, sectarian visionaries. Rather, like our father Abraham, we are encouraged to become even more involved with life and mankind. We are called to live a life that is filled with the presence of God. A life that is loving, and constantly and creatively expanding. A life that is joyful and filled to its fullness in our Lord, Yeshua; for the sake of His Name and the extension of God's Kingdom in the earth.

Lekh Lekha, Once More!

Abraham faces his most difficult test at the end of this parasha, when God tells him once more: "*Lekh lekha (Go forth)*". This time he is to go forth and take his beloved son Isaac to a "*mountain I will show you*" (22:2) and to offer him there as a sacrifice. How does Abraham respond? Just as before, he hurries to obey—no questions asked! What God was asking challenged Abraham's thinking and his understanding of God, and was certainly contrary to Abraham's expectations. He proved, however, that his overriding priority was to trust his God and quickly to obey His clear command, no matter how mysterious or confusing it appeared.

All of God's tests, as a loving Father, are intended to strengthen and elevate His children—to lift us to greater heights than we otherwise would attain. Abraham, quite understandably, could have refused this fearful command, but through his obedience he ensures that his lineage will bring forth the Messiah. In response God reaffirms His promise to Abraham:

> *And all the nations of the earth will be blessed through your seed because you have obeyed my voice* (22:18).

Abraham's willingness to obey God's command to sacrifice Isaac indicates in fact that he is willing to sacrifice himself. All his hopes and promise for the future are bound up in Isaac. The very existence of God's people, the household of faith, seems to be at stake. Yet we see, as the narrative unfolds, that mankind's journey from the valley of Shinar and the Tower of Babel now progresses to the heights of *Har Moriah*, Mount Moriah—the mountain of the LORD, the place He chooses to place His Name forever.

The place of Abraham's sacrifice becomes the place of the ultimate sacrifice of God's own Beloved Son. In His sacrifice we lay our broken lives down, and by His wounds we are made whole and can walk in newness of life as beloved of God (Galatians 6:15). We hold to the promise that the Lamb of God will one day reign gloriously over all the earth from this same place, when His throne is established on the holy Mount in Jerusalem.

> *Let this be recorded for a generation to come (*Hebrew: *dor acharon*—the last generation*), so that a people yet unborn may praise the* LORD*: that he looked down from his holy height, ...to hear the groans of the prisoners, to set free those who were doomed to die; that men may declare in Zion the name of the* LORD*, and in Jerusalem his praise, when peoples gather together, and kingdoms, to worship the* LORD" (RSV, Psalm 102:18-22).

---

[1] *101 Famous Poems*, An Anthology compiled by Roy J. Cook, 9.

Chayei Sarah - חיי שרה

Sarah's Life

Genesis 23:1–25:18; 1 Kings 1:1–31; Philippians 2:5–11

The *parasha* opens with an unusual breakdown of Sarah's life: 100 years, 20 years and 7 years. In reverse this represents and includes four phases of life—childhood, adolescence, adulthood and elderly maturity. According to the Sages, Sarah carried the beauty of her childhood into young womanhood and she retained the modest innocence of a woman of twenty all the days of her life. They propose that true modesty and godly innocence is achieved when one has faced and struggled with the sensuality and passion of youth and has emerged victorious, having gained control over it.

The Life of Sarah

Although the context of the portion is Sarah's death and burial, her life is referred to twice in the first verse. Also, when Abraham's death is mentioned later, we read: *The days of Abraham's life, which he lived* (25:7). This seems to highlight the fact that the couple truly lived their lives fully—both physically and spiritually. Their lives were filled with the highest purpose and most noble of goals: to share their knowledge of God and His ways with others and to practice *chesed,* deeds of loving-kindness, at every opportunity. Each of their days was devoted to serving God in righteousness. As a result, their days counted for eternity. They truly 'lived' and their deeds left an imprint on generations to come.

The *parasha* records the account of Abraham's purchase of a piece of land in Canaan from Ephron the Hittite, which includes a cave for burial and the surrounding field. As well as the record of King David's purchase of Ornan the Jebusite's threshing floor, which was to become the site of the Temple (1 Chronicles 22:21-25), there is another account of the legal purchase of land in the Scriptures—Jeremiah's purchase of a field (Jeremiah 32:6ff). Abraham's transaction occurs well before the establishment of Israel's nationhood and Jeremiah's is undertaken on the verge of the Babylonian exile. Both are God-inspired acts of faith.

A Wife for Isaac

In another act of faith, Abraham sends his trusted and faithful servant to find a wife for his son, Isaac. Interestingly, in an account filled with names, the man he entrusts with this highly important mission is not named. Although he is of high standing and responsibility in Abraham's household, he introduces himself and is referred to as "Abraham's servant." This is an indication of the character and the true humility of the man. It also indicates how far those in Abraham's household of faith have come from the self-centered generation of the Tower of Babel who desired only to "make a name" for themselves (Genesis 11:4).

Abraham is adamant on two issues: first that Isaac is not to marry a Canaanite woman (24:3) but rather one from his own family, and secondly that Isaac always must remain in the land God had promised to Abraham and his offspring (24:7). We are given a hint at God's hand in this marriage at the end of last week's *parasha*. Some time after the intense challenge of the binding of Isaac, it is recorded that Abraham was informed that his brother Nahor's wife, Milcah, had borne him eight sons. The youngest son, Bethuel, had become the father of Rebekah (22:23). *Rivkah*, her name in Hebrew, is the only girl listed amongst Nahor's children and grandchildren, indicating that she has a significant role to play in God's purposes in the unfolding narrative of His chosen people.

When Abraham's servant arrives at his destination, he rests his camels near a well on the outskirts of the town. It is near evening and the women soon will be coming to draw water. He knows he cannot rely on his own judgment in this vital search and he offers a fervent prayer for success to the Lord, the God of Abraham (24:12). He then also petitions God to show *chesed*, lovingkindness, to his master. We glean from the biblical text that since the ultimate test of God's command to sacrifice his beloved son and the subsequent death of Sarah, the light in both Abraham and Isaac's lives has dimmed. The one who is renowned for his *chesed,* Abraham, is now in urgent need of the *chesed* of God.

Quick to Serve

Abraham's servant prays that he will be given a specific sign of God's choice of a wife for Isaac. When he asks for a drink of water, the maiden will reply, "*Drink, and I'll water your camels too*" (24:14). How instant God is to answer the prayer of a fervent, unselfish heart! The next verse reads: *Before he had finished praying, Rivkah came out with her jar on her shoulder.* We are told that she was very beautiful and a virgin, but the test of her character remained.

The account that follows contains encouraging echoes of the character and spirit of our father Abraham, particularly in that she is quick to serve. The servant *hurries* to meet her; she *quickly* lowers the jar; she *quickly* empties the jar, and *runs* back to the well. He is watching her intently. She accomplishes the demanding task of drawing and pouring enough water for all his camels—a large amount! He is impressed enough to pursue the matter and he asks her whose daughter she is and if the family could provide accommodation for the night. Her answers "clinch the deal". She is Bethuel's daughter; and her generous offer of hospitality, including feed for the camels, causes him to "*bow down and worship the LORD*" (24:26). He gives praise to the One who has faithfully directed him to the home of Abraham's family and, it appears, to God's choice of a wife for Isaac.

And He Loved Her

We learn from the statement of her brother Laban, "Let us call the maiden and ask as to her desire" (24:57) that Rebekah's consent to the marriage was necessary. Laban also demonstrates the custom of blessing the bride. His words are still recited to the bride at Jewish weddings today, before she walks to the *chuppah* (wedding canopy):

> *Our sister, be the mother of thousands of ten thousands; and may your descendants possess the gate of those who hate them* (24:60).

Rebekah then sets out with Abraham's servant on the journey that will result in the joining of her destiny with that of Isaac.

The marriage of Isaac and Rebekah was not based on love and passion for one another, but on the will of their Father God. In a godly marriage the wedding is not the culmination but rather the beginning of true love.

> *And Isaac took Rebekah...*—he received her, there was mutual consent and attraction—*and she became his wife ... and he loved her* (24:67).

The marriage covenant, like all God's covenants, is intended for life and blessing. It is the original design and chief means of reflecting His image and sanctifying His Name in this world.

In a godly marriage relationship the fruit of love, righteousness and self-control is *shalom*—the blessed state of peace and wholeness that our Father in heaven desires for all His children. The shalom that is demonstrated in the harmony and unity of the *echad* (oneness) of God Himself.

Toldot - תולדות

Generations

Genesis 25:19–28:9; Malachi 1:1–2:7; Romans 9:6–13

The name of this week's parasha *Toldot* means generations, or literally 'birthings' (from the root word *leidah*, birth). From the beginning, when Adam and Eve are expelled from the Garden and God tells them: *Be fruitful and multiply* (1:22), the biblical narrative describes a prolific ebb and flow of life—a stream of begettings! However, in the midst of this flow sudden pauses appear: "the interruption of barrenness"[1]. Each of the beloved wives of the patriarchs, Sarah, Rebekah and Rachel is initially unable to bear children. This issue is particularly arresting in the face of the promise: *To you and your descendents I will give this Land* (12:7).

It seems that God desires to draw attention to the fact that theirs are not regular, ordinary births—the result of the will and desire of the couples involved. They are, in fact, miraculous; a result of God's divine ordination for His divine purposes. They demonstrate the supernatural intervention of God Himself in the lives of His chosen people, and are somehow related to the land He had promised them. *The whole land of Canaan...I will give to you and your descendents after you, and I will be their God* (17:8).

Jacob and Esau - Sibling Rivalry

Another interruption in the flow and harmony of familial history is the immediate emergence of sibling rivalry between the first brothers, Cain and Abel. So bitter is Cain's resentment of God's favor towards Abel that it results in the first murder. The account of rivalry and murderous anger between Esau and Jacob is of even greater importance in the narrative as it erupts in the patriarchal line. The outcome is pivotal to the future of God's people. We saw it first in the contention surrounding Isaac and Ishmael and now, even more intensely, between Jacob and Esau.

The complex question of Rebekah and Jacob's deception of Isaac in order to procure the birthright or spiritual leadership of the family is one of ongoing debate and commentary. Why was it necessary to enter into this deception? Why could Rebekah not simply have explained her view to Isaac that, although he was technically the elder of the twins, Esau was neither fit nor worthy to inherit the right to be one of the "founding fathers" of the people of God? Rebekah had painfully experienced the wrestling of the twins in her womb and had cried to the Lord for understanding. His clear answer was: *Two nations are in your womb... And the elder shall serve the younger* (25:23).

In addition, Esau had already caused his parents great distress by marrying two Hittite women (26:35). Isaac must have recalled the efforts of his father Abraham in finding him a non-pagan wife in accordance with God's command. Esau, however, had shown blatant disregard for the wishes of both God and his parents.

And yet we are told: *Now Isaac loved Esau, because he did eat of his venison, and Rebekah loved Jacob* (25:28). It appears that Isaac's affection is based on Esau's provision of the delicious venison stew that he loves. Isaac had been a quiet man of the fields and now he is old and feeble and *his eyes were dimmed and he could not see* (27:1). Thus, he no doubt delights in his strong, outdoor son, who was a hunter, more than he does in his quiet, studious son who helps his mother and *remained in the tents* (25:27).

Jacob surely yearns for the acceptance and affection of his father. In taking on the identity of Esau, in accord with his mother's plan, perhaps he sees an opportunity to experience his father's affirmation and embrace, however fleeting the moment. Indeed the deception is soon exposed and Jacob must flee for his life from Esau's wrath. God subsequently leads him on a long and event-filled journey through which he discovers the fullness of his own unique identity. As Rabbi Shlomo Riskin comments:

> But Jacob's journey will only be completed, and the Lord will only [fully] become his God, when he eventually returns in peace—and is at peace with—his father's house, and as Jacob-Israel not Jacob-Esau![2]

Isaac - A Bridge and a Balance

Toldot is the only parasha that covers the time in which all three forefathers were alive in the world. Each one was called to serve the Lord in his own distinctive way. Although much less is written about Isaac he provides the balance and the bridge, as it were, between the strong personalities of his father Abraham and his son Jacob.

Abraham was primarily noted for his *chesed* (lovingkindness). He was the quintessential example of the values of generosity, hospitality, and social commitment. As Rabbi Yitzchak Sufrin, of the Highgate Synagogue in London, aptly describes:

[Abraham's] home and heart were always open to any wayfarer, to offer food, drink, companionship and guidance.

The Sages of Israel attribute to Jacob the primary characteristic of *emet* (truth) due to his devotion to the study of God's ways. He constantly wrestled to discover the truth and he overcame.

Isaac, they consider, personified *yir'at HaShem* (fear/reverence of God). This quality is the vital balance between love and truth. Love must be restrained and disciplined by the awe of God in order to produce self-control, as well as the other fruit of the Spirit: love, joy, peace, patience, kindness, goodness, faithfulness, gentleness (Galatians 5:22-23). If not, extreme kindness and tolerance can promote self-indulgence and lawlessness (*Torah*-lessness).

On the other hand, an over-emphasis on truth can lead to self-righteousness and legalism, which in the extreme leads to undue selfishness and hardness of heart. Isaac represents the balance between love and truth that is enabled by reverential awe of God.

Love, Truth, Awe

The ideal—*chesed ve'emet*, love and truth, bound together by the fear of God—produces true godly righteousness. The perfect balance of all three is demonstrated in the person and life of *Yeshua mi'Natzeret*, Jesus of Nazareth. In reaching out to embrace the world in self-sacrificial love, He embodies the *chesed* of God exhibited by Abraham. He is the fullness of truth, as sought after and lived by Jacob-Israel, and He is the superb balance of them both, illustrated in the restraint, discipline and obedient awe of Isaac.

A beautiful corresponding description is found at the conclusion of the *haftarah* regarding the characteristics of the "messenger of the Lord of hosts":

> *The instruction of truth (torat emet) was in his mouth, and no wrong was found on his lips. He walked with me in shalom [peace and wholeness] and uprightness [love-based righteousness and integrity], and he turned many from iniquity* (Malachi 2:6).

---

1 Quote from lecture by Avivah Gottlieb Zornberg, author of *The Beginnings of Desire, Reflections on Genesis.*

2 Rabbi Shlomo Riskin, *Torah Lights, Genesis Confronts Life, Love and Family,* 169.

Va'yetze - ויצא
And He Went Out

Genesis 28:10–32:3; Hosea 12:12–14:10;
John 1:43–51

The first verse of this intriguing, multi-layered *parasha* is a very direct, purposeful statement: *And Jacob went out from Beersheva and went towards Haran* (28:10). He knows why he is leaving—at the command of his parents, with the dual purpose of escaping his brother's wrath and to seek a wife for himself from his grandfather Abraham's family (28:3). He also knows his destination. His is an intentional setting out—*yetzeh*—unlike Abraham's going out—*lekh*—in a response of faith to God's command.

Jacob's Encounter

The next verse describes how he suddenly arrives at a place. The literal translation of the Hebrew text is more dramatic. *Va'yifga ba'makom.* "And he collided with the place." It was a startling, unexpected encounter. *Yifga* suggests a dynamic encounter with an object that is traveling towards oneself.[1] A word in modern Hebrew from the same root is *paga*, to hit (as in "to hit the target"), and a word familiar today, *pigua*, a terrorist attack.

As the redeemed of the Lord we move forward in our lives, planning in faith and hope towards our goals and desires, which we trust are in accordance with His will. But sudden, unexpected events can occur that interrupt our plans and disrupt the harmonious pattern we anticipated. They startle and shake us. On later reflection, however, we realize that unpleasant shocks can result in great good. We are given the opportunity to grow. They stir up the spirit and life within us and demand that we seek and reach out for God. They stretch the limits of our existence and our lives are changed.

In her rich, imaginative commentary[2], Avivah Gottlieb Zornberg explores the idea of Jacob's dispossession of his former life. Before he set out from his father's house, Isaac blessed him with the blessing of Abraham: *May He give the blessing of Abraham to you and your seed, that you may take possession of the land of your sojournings, which God gave to Abraham* (28:3-4). Part of the heritage of the children of Abraham is to be sojourners and strangers in exile before they become inheritors of God's Land of promise. This implies a sense of dissatisfaction with the kingdoms of the world—a searching and wandering on the earth, while one's soul finds rest in God alone[3].

It appears that Esau was quite comfortable and settled; enjoying his life among the pagan Hittites. Jacob's life, however, displays an element of the emotional and spiritual heritage of "Abraham's seed"—an unsettledness that impels one to question. There is an awareness of the need to go through many stages of spiritual growth, a growth in wisdom and understanding, to become 'more'. The true children of Abraham have an instinctive God-given awareness that there is 'more'. They are thus prompted by the Spirit of God to actively pursue it and not to settle for the 'less' the world offers.

The apostle Paul underscores this concept in his exhortation to the Colossians (1:9-10):

> *We have not ceased to pray for you, asking that you may be filled with the knowledge of his will in all spiritual wisdom and*

understanding, to lead a life worthy of the L*ORD*, *fully pleasing to him, bearing fruit in every good work and increasing in the knowledge of God.*

The Stone Pillow

Once Jacob "hits the wall," as it were, he can go no further. The sun has set, so he decides to sleep. He takes *one of the stones of the place* (28:11) to use as a pillow. Tradition holds that the place of this encounter is Mount Moriah—the same place where Abraham prepared to sacrifice his son Isaac when God stayed his hand and provided a ram. Some commentators suggest that the stone Jacob used could have been one of the stones of the altar of sacrifice upon which his own father had been bound and offered as a sacrifice. Now he rests his head upon it and God once again reveals Himself.

This is God's first proclamation of His desire to come down and to establish His dwelling place among His people on earth. This very place of sacrifice is in fact destined to become the site of His glorious Temple. It will be the place of the ultimate sacrifice of His Son and Messiah, and the foundation of His house of prayer for all nations.

As he sleeps, Jacob dreams. He sees a ladder connecting heaven and earth. The angels of God are ascending and descending on it. And *hineh* (behold) the LORD stood above it (28:12-13). One of Israel's esteemed teachers of Torah, Nechama Leibowitz (Jerusalem, 1905-1997), points out that according to the Midrash, *Tanchumah*[4]:

> Jacob's dream depicts the rise and fall of nations and their cultures on the arena of world history.

Jacob's ladder can thus be seen as the ladder of history, which is grounded upon Israel, who are witnesses to the rise and fall of many mighty kingdoms. We see that:

The LORD stands at its top as the master of history, assuring us that pride and despotism will be brought low, until His sovereignty alone is recognized at the end of days.[5]

Jacob's response when he awakes (both a spiritual and physical awakening) is one of awe and recognition: *Surely the LORD is in this place, and I knew it not!* (28:16).

Strangely enough, it is in the darkness, in the uncertainty and fear of his journey into night, that Jacob finds *ha'Makom*—the Place of truth—the ground where he begins the discovery of his true identity. He is not bound as his father was but is free to stand and bless the Lord in this holy place. One finds an echo of this in Psalm 134:1, *Come bless the LORD, all you servants of the LORD, who stand by night in the House of the LORD.*

Jacob dedicates this place and names it Bethel—*Beit-El*, House of God (28:19).

Deception and Deliverance

Jacob experiences another dark night. At the moment of his greatest joy, his marriage to his beloved Rachel, he discovers after the wedding night that Leah has been substituted in her place. Jacob is struck by ripples of his own deception. Although it was part of her father's scheme and greed, it was also in her yearning to be loved and accepted by Jacob that Leah had assumed her sister's identity. Jacob's eyes were blinded in the darkness, just as Isaac could not see when Jacob had assumed his brother's identity and answered to Esau's name. Laban reaffirms the link in the morning when Jacob confronts him on the deception and he replies: "*It is not so done in our place, to give the younger before the first born!*" (29:26). Jacob suffers as his true love is interrupted and spoiled by the deception. And Leah suffers when she does not win his love. The text states that initially he "hated" her (29:31). No doubt she was a constant reminder of the negative cause of his exile.

At the conclusion of the *parasha* we find Jacob after twenty years of exile at the border of his homeland once again. He is returning, as the Lord had promised, with much increase, and *the angels of God met him* (32:2). His God, the God of Abraham and Isaac, had been with him, and kept him, and was bringing him back to His Land and His House—*ha'Makom*—the Place where His Name would be established forever. This will be the very Place where the Almighty God will be glorified when His Son, Yeshua the Messiah, will reign as King of kings over all the earth at the end of days—as the apostle John records in his prophetic vision of that time:

> *And I saw the holy city, [renewed] Jerusalem, coming down out of heaven from God, prepared as a bride adorned for her husband; and I heard a loud voice from the throne saying,*
>
> *"Behold, the dwelling of God is with men. He will dwell with them, and they shall be His people, and God himself will be with them; He will wipe away every tear from their eyes, and death shall be no more, neither shall there be mourning nor crying nor pain any more, for the former things have passed away."*
>
> *And He who sat upon the throne said, "Behold, I make all things new."*

---

1 Avivah G. Zornberg, *The Beginning of Desire, Reflections on Genesis*, 187.

2 Ibid.

3 Psalm 116:7

4 Nechama Leibowitz (Jerusalem, Israel, 1905-1997), *Genesis*, 299.

5 Ibid., 300.

Va'yishlach - וישלח

And He Sent

Genesis 32:4–36:43; Hosea 11:7–12:12;
Matthew 26:36–42

The portion this week describes the dramatic event of Jacob's return to his homeland. His return is not one of joyous celebration and hopeful anticipation. Rather, he is greatly afraid and distressed at the prospect of once again encountering his brother Esau. Twenty years have lapsed since he left his home to escape Esau's murderous rage. The daunting story of the first siblings, Cain and Abel, may be echoing in his mind. He is, no doubt, plagued by fearful questions. Does his brother still intend to kill him? How can he defend himself and his family? Will he need to kill in self defense?

Deal with Fear

Jacob does not give in to his fear but takes positive steps to protect himself and his family from the possible evil intentions of his brother. We can learn from Jacob's method of dealing with his distressful dilemma. He faces the problem and takes positive action.

First, he proactively makes contact with Esau. The first verse of the *parasha* tells us that Jacob *yishlach malakhim* (sent messengers) ahead of him to his brother, bearing words of goodwill. Interestingly, the Hebrew word *malakhim* also means angels. This could indicate that the earthly messengers were accompanied by heaven-sent angels who provided God's protection and favor. The earthly envoys return with no specific word from Esau, which is not encouraging. In addition, they report the disconcerting fact that he is approaching accompanied by a large 'welcoming party' of four hundred men (32:6).

After making responsible preparations for his family and flocks, Jacob turns to God in prayer (32:10). He proclaims his own unworthiness, reminds God of His promise to him, and prays for deliverance. Just as Abraham and Isaac were men of prayer, so is Jacob. These are the first recorded words of a formal, personal prayer in the Bible, which highlights its significance. We are reminded that prayer is a major priority when we are faced with any of life's challenges.

Jacob then sends substantial gifts to Esau as tangible proof that he is returning in peace (32:14-16). As a result of his careful preparations and the confirming presence and protection of God, we read later that Jacob arrives safely (*shalem*—in peace, unharmed and whole) in the city of Shechem.

Jacob's Struggle - Our Struggle?

Before re-entering the Land, Jacob experiences another mysterious encounter in the night. It is reminiscent of his collision with *haMakom*, the Place, which had occurred during his escape journey. The encounter is introduced by the verse, *And Jacob remained alone, and a man wrestled with him* (32:24). Many questions are raised. For example: Who is his anonymous assailant? What bearing has this on his anticipated encounter with Esau? Is it intended as a blessing or as punishment, or a warning? The text offers no clear answers but the outcome of the struggle, we discover, is that Jacob prevails. He consequently receives a blessing, and he is awarded a new name—*Israel.*[1]

The nature of the confrontation, including the identity of the man Jacob wrestles with, has been interpreted on many levels. It can reflect one's spiritual struggle with God, the struggle within oneself, and one's struggle with opposing forces. The last is a classic *midrashic* or homiletic answer, speculating that the opponent is Esau's guardian angel whom Jacob must overcome on a spiritual level in order to gain victory and peace on a physical level.

Avivah Gottlieb Zornberg [2] notes, however, that according to another midrashic tradition the man/angel has come not for any hostile purpose but to "save and rescue him," to show Jacob how to become Israel—how to be a person of power and authority with the capacity to confront, to passionately wrestle and to overcome. This concept can be applied on an historic level to the nation of Israel that emerges from Jacob's descendents.

The Sages also suggest that this incident reflects Israel's future struggles with nations that will assail and attempt to overthrow and destroy God's people. Jacob's victory provides "the vision of the eventual triumph of Jerusalem over Rome." [3] Just as the Lord promised Abraham in the Covenant of the Pieces[4] the descendants of Jacob, Israel, would be the bearers of God's Presence in history and would be at the center of its outworking.

On a personal level we can understand that God Himself confronts and challenges us, His children. At times He encounters us face-to-face and wrestles with us in order to present us with the reality of our higher "self"—the unique one-of-a-kind self He ordained and created in His image—the "you" that was in His mind from before the beginning of time. The desire of the Father's heart is that we grow more and more into that image, for our own blessing and in order to more clearly reflect His glory in the earth.

We may consider that one of the reasons He sent Yeshua, His Son, into the earth was to challenge and teach us about our true "new creation" selves. By example, He leads us in the way of the Father's holiness and by impartation we are empowered to walk in the power of His Spirit of holiness. As the apostle Paul encourages:

> *...you have put off the old nature with its practices and have put on the new nature, which is being renewed in knowledge after the image of its Creator.*[5]

Love Your Enemy?

A deep appreciation of the truth that every individual is created in the image of God, and is therefore worthy of our respect, attention and loving care, can transform one's attitude towards and communication with others. Our perception of enemies is also affected, as Yeshua exhorts us in Matthew 5:44-45,

> *I say to you, Love your enemies and pray for those who persecute you, so that you may be sons of your Father who is in heaven; for He makes His sun rise on the evil and on the good, and sends rain on the just and on the unjust.*

It seems this is a lesson Jacob learned from his encounter, for when he finally comes face to face with his brother he says, "*To see your face is like seeing the face of God*" (33:10). If we allow our authentic, true self to respond to the image of God in another, no matter how deeply it is hidden, we are afforded the opportunity to encounter God in every person He brings into our life's journey. In so doing we encourage one another to become more true to His image within us,. Then, as the light of His Presence shines forth all the more in our lives, peace between 'brothers' can be restored.

[1] Dov Chaiken, friend and Hebrew mentor, observed that the 29th November, 1947— the day the United Nations General Assembly voted for the partition of Palestine—was a Saturday (Shabbat) and the Torah reading in synagogues world-wide was this parasha, where Jacob's name is changed to Israel.

[2] Avivah Gottlieb Zornberg, The Beginning of Desire, Reflections on Genesis, 234.

[3] Ibid., 231.

[4] Genesis 15:9-21

[5] Colossians 3:9-10

Va'yeishev - וישב

And He Dwelt

Genesis 37:1–40:23; Amos 2:6 – 3:8, 9:11–15;
John 10:22–30

And Jacob dwelt (va'yeishev Ya'akov) in the land where his father had sojourned, the land of Canaan (37:1). The Hebrew title of the parasha denotes settling down. Many troubles had beset Jacob since his return to the Land—particularly the rape of his daughter Dinah and the subsequent vengeful attack by his sons Shimon and Levi, and thereafter the death of his beloved wife Rachel. Jacob is now seeking to settle down in peace.

The narrative resumes in verse 2, however, with an immediate reference to his son Joseph and we come to realize in the ensuing drama that Jacob's peace is illusive. By the end of the chapter his life is *tarof toraf* (torn to pieces), his peace is shattered by the disappearance and imagined fate of his precious son (37:33).

Jacob is a representative of the righteous who desire harmony—the beauty and order of life as God intended—but he must again face the shock and reality of the inherent disease and disorder of this fallen world.

Brother versus Brother

The multi-faceted, colorful story of Joseph is ever fresh and challenging. We are introduced to Joseph, firstborn of Rachel, as a precocious young man who tattletales on his brothers (37:2). His father, Jacob, loves him more than all his children and *he made him a coat of many colors* (37:13). Unfortunately, young Joseph is not wise and he proudly parades his ornate coat (outer garment, literally robe or tunic) before his brothers. He also, without hesitation, shares his clear dreams of his family bowing to him in homage (37:5-11). His ingenuous attitude and their father's favoritism infuriate the brothers to the point of hatred, *and they could not speak peaceably to him* (37:4).

Rabbi Shlomo Riskin comments that the Sages lay a measure of responsibility on Jacob for the ensuing tragedy, as is written in the Talmud (Shabbat10b):

> A person must never favor one child among the others; because of a piece of material [fancy clothing] ... his brothers became jealous of him and the matter degenerated until our forefathers were forced to descend to Egypt.[1]

Jacob later pays a heavy price for this misjudgment, when he bears the grief of believing for twenty-two years that his beloved son suffered a cruel death.

We see the biblical theme of sibling rivalry leading to violence once again played out when Jacob innocently sends Joseph to see *whether all is well with his brothers, and well with the flock* (37:14). This involves a long journey from Hebron to Shechem, which causes one to wonder why Jacob sent his favored son alone on such a mission?

In Shechem[2], he is informed that his brothers have moved on to Dothan to find pasture. The brothers see Joseph approaching from afar. United in their hatred against this "Lord of the Dreams" (*ba'al ha'chalomot*, 37:20) they spontaneously plot to kill him and fling him into one of the pits nearby. Only one brother, Reuben, speaks out against shedding his blood and suggests they throw him into the pit alive. To give him the benefit of the doubt, one can presume that he plans to rescue him from there and to return him to his father. When

Joseph arrives, no doubt weary and hungry after his journey, the brothers strip him of his ornamental, colorful robe and drop him into a pit, one that fortunately was empty of water. In a callous gesture, oblivious to his likely cries for mercy and help, they then *...sat down to eat bread* (37:25).

A caravan of traders en route to Egypt comes by and Judah suggests selling Joseph to avoid having his blood on their hands. The others agree and, without Reuben's knowledge, they sell him for twenty pieces of silver. To cover their betrayal they slaughter a kid, dip Joseph's robe in its blood and return it to Jacob, who is convinced that his son has been torn (*tarof toraf*) and devoured by a wild beast. While Jacob bitterly mourns the death of his favorite son, Joseph is sold in Egypt as a slave to Potiphar, a royal official in the court of Pharaoh. The plans and purposes of the mighty God of Israel are unfolding.

Heaven and Earth

Dreams play an important part in Joseph's life and mission. The content of his two initial dreams contribute to his brothers' envy and hatred of him. In his first dream he sees a harvested field of wheat and his brothers' sheaves are bowing down to his sheaf. His second dream is set in the heavens and the sun, moon and eleven stars are bowing down to him (37:7-9).

Even his father rebukes him as he recounts the second dream; as Jews they know that one only bows down to God Himself. His brothers are incensed. Does this upstart think he is God? Here we have a clear foreshadowing of the reaction to Yeshua by some of His Jewish brethren, particularly the less-than-perfect authority figures in the Temple. Yeshua, too, was betrayed by his brothers for pieces of silver and was handed over to strangers. In fact, the Sages of Israel attribute the destruction of the Second Temple, with its tragic aftermath of the exile, to the sin of causeless hatred of one's brothers.

Jacob carefully guards the dreams of Joseph in his heart (37:11). We can remember that his life also was impacted by a vivid dream—the ladder that united heaven and earth and connected the land and the stars. Jacob knew God was with him and that these God-inspired dreams had Messianic import. Did he, perhaps with prophetic foresight, understand that Joseph somehow represented a chosen, beloved and specially anointed Son—*Mashiach ben Yosef* , Messiah son of Joseph?[3] The Son in and through whom God Himself would mightily act to effect reconciliation between heaven and earth.

This beloved Son would bring familial and universal redemption and establish a renewed, dynamic, life-giving connection between God and man. In Him the relationship between the Father and His family, Israel, is destined to find its intended fulfillment. This same *Mashiach-El*, Lamb-of-God Messiah, will one day reign as the Lion of Judah, the King of kings, and will bring to fruition for all nations the true *Shalom* (wholeness and peace) for which Jacob and all his descendants long with hopeful anticipation.

---

[1] Rabbi Shlomo Riskin, *Torah Lights, Genesis Confronts Life, Love and Family*, 223.

[2] Shechem is a key city in Israel, ancient and modern. It was the place of Joseph's burial when his bones were carried back from Egypt. In our time, his tomb in Nablus (Shechem) has been targeted and desecrated by the PLO.

[3] Jewish tradition speaks of two Messiahs: Messiah son of Joseph (*Mashiach ben Yosef*), the suffering servant, and Messiah son of David (*Mashiach ben David*), of the tribe of Judah, the King of kings.

Miketz - מקץ
At the End

Genesis 41:1–44:17; 1 Kings 3:15–4:1;
1 Corinthians 2:9–16

It happened at the end (miketz) of two years to the day (41:1).

The opening verse indicates that God's timing is very specific. An ending marks the beginning of something new. The time has come for the start of a chain of events that will result in great fruitfulness in Joseph's life. It also, however, will usher in the fulfillment of the prophecy to Abraham that his descendents would be exiled and persecuted.

Joseph's life in Egypt, up to this point, has been dramatic. He was imprisoned after Potiphar's wife unfairly accused him of attempting to seduce her. While in prison, Joseph's sterling character earned him the favor of the jailer. He had also accurately interpreted significant dreams of two fellow prisoners, the baker and the cupbearer of Pharaoh's court. As Joseph foretold, the cupbearer was declared innocent and released, but despite Joseph's pleas to speak on his behalf the cupbearer forgot him. Exactly two years later, to the day, Joseph is remembered and *they rushed him up from the dungeon* (41:14).

God's acts of intervention and redemption usually happen very quickly and unexpectedly after what seems a long and often painful season of waiting. Similarly, according to Malachi 3:1, the coming of *Mashiach ben David,* Messiah son of David, at the end of days will be sudden and hasty, at an exact time known only to the Father.

More Dreams

Pharaoh was greatly disturbed by his dreams of seven lean and sickly cows consuming seven sturdy, healthy cows and seven thin, blighted ears of grain swallowing up seven plump and healthy ears. When the wise men of the court could offer no interpretation, the cupbearer shared his story and Joseph was summoned. In his encounter with Joseph, Pharaoh recognizes that the Spirit of God is within this young foreigner. He is so impressed with his clear interpretation of the dreams and with his wisdom that he places Joseph in charge of all Egypt, second only to himself (41:31-48).

In addition, he gives Joseph a new name, *Tzaph'nat-panei'ach.* Rabbi Hertz[1] records the explanation of Egyptologists that *Tzaph'nat* means 'food-man' (or bread-man) and *panei'ach*, 'of life'. In the light of Joseph as a precursor of Yeshua, *Mashiach ben Yosef*, the appellation of 'Man of the bread of life' is interesting.

Also of interest is the fact that Joseph is now thirty years old (41:46). This is the age at which Jewish men could enter priestly service at the Temple and the age at which Yeshua began His earthly ministry. Nevertheless, it is a very young age to be awarded the highest governmental position in a powerful nation and to bear the responsibility of running the affairs of the country. This testifies to Joseph's God-given wisdom and grace and emphasizes that, when God so wills, even the forces of nature and politics must yield to make the impossible possible.

Joseph's Sons

Pharaoh presents Joseph with a wife—Asenath, the daughter of the priest of On (41:45). Hertz records[2] that the city of On, later called Heliopolis, was near Cairo and was the center of

Sun worship. The famous landmark on the Thames Embankment in London, Cleopatra's Needle, originally stood in On!

We can assume that Asenath learned from Joseph and, in the knowledge of the God of Abraham, Isaac, and Jacob, adopted his spiritual beliefs and moral standards. Consequently, their children were raised to be the models after which Jewish parents to this day bless their sons every Shabbat: *May God make you like Ephraim and Manasseh* (48:20).

Manasseh (*Mena'sheh*) means: "God has made me forget all my hardship." Joseph recognized that all the hardship he had endured—the betrayal by his brothers, the separation from his father and homeland, being sold into slavery, his unjust imprisonment—all were part of God's master plan to prepare him for the position in which he now finds himself. Therefore Joseph is grateful for all his hardships and he is able to forgive his brothers fully.

Ephraim (*Efrai'yim*) means: "God has made me fruitful in the land of my suffering." In spite of his success and prosperity, Joseph continues to view Egypt as the land of his suffering. He never forgets that he is a son of Israel, and that God's Promised Land will always remain his homeland. His choice of Hebrew names for his sons gives evidence of this.

The paradoxical juxtaposition of fruitfulness and suffering in Joseph's life is clearly depicted in their names. This can encourage us. When one's life is in God's hands it is possible to be fruitful, to be a life-giver, even in a place of suffering and alienation. Joseph is raised by God from the pit of suffering, from the place of rejection, negation, and affliction as a slave and a prisoner, to become the sustainer of life for many nations.

Galut ve'Geulah - Exile and Redemption

The central and profound biblical theme of exile and redemption continues to build with the arrival of Joseph's ten brothers. In the face of a dire famine that strikes the entire region, they seek grain in Egypt. When they approach Joseph for aid he immediately recognizes them, *but they knew him not* (42:8). He appears to be fully Egyptian in dress, language and name.

Joseph employs an intricate series of tests for his brothers, to establish if they have experienced any remorse for their previous hateful deeds against him. He also attempts to discover the fate of his father and younger brother, Benjamin. In response to his harsh reaction, Joseph hears his brothers' comments: "*Alas, we are being punished on account of our brother, because we looked on at his anguish, yet would not listen as he pleaded with us*" (42:21-23). Joseph is overcome with emotion and turns aside to weep. He later weeps again when, according to his instructions, Benjamin is brought before him. Publicly, however, he maintains his impassive, royal demeanor. The final test comes when he orders the ten to return to their father without Benjamin. Will they abandon him as they had Joseph?

At that moment Judah steps forward and, in a most eloquent and moving plea, offers himself in place of Benjamin. He explains that he cannot bear to witness his father's grief at the loss of a second son. Joseph can no longer restrain himself. He orders all the court attendants to withdraw, and with no one else present Joseph reveals his identity to his brothers. His weeping then erupts so loudly that it echoes through the palace. His brothers, no doubt, are dumbfounded. Joseph assuages any fear of recrimination with his words, "*It was to save life that God sent me ahead of you...to ensure your survival on earth... It was not you who sent me here, but God...*" (45:4-8).

Avivah Zornberg underscores this truth in her commentary:

> From God's perspective, he had been just where he was meant to be, swallowed up, giving and saving life... Out of the brokenness has come a rethinking of the past, a redeeming of the past, a hope for wholeness in the house of Jacob.[3]

This dramatic reunion can be seen as a prophetic portrayal of the glorious reconciliation that will occur at the appointed time between Yeshua and His alienated Jewish brothers. Through the last two thousand years He has been unrecognizable to the Jewish people in His 'gentile' garb, as it were, often with the identity of a Christian Conqueror. But the day will come, when hearts will soften in repentance towards the Father, and Yeshua will reveal His full identity as a Jewish brother and Messiah. The past will be redeemed and new life and true shalom will burst forth like a fountain, and the whole house of Jacob—indeed all the descendants of Abraham—will move fully and exultantly from Exile to Redemption.

> *On that day living waters shall flow out from Jerusalem... And the* Lord *will become king over all the earth; on that day the* Lord *will be one and his name one* (Zechariah 14:8-9).

---

[1] Rabbi Dr. J.H. Hertz, *Pentateuch and Haftorahs*, Second Edition, 158.

[2] Ibid., 158.

[3] Avivah Gottlieb Zorberg, *The Beginning of Desire, Reflections on Genesis*, 311.

Va'yigash - ויגש
And Came Near

Genesis 44:18–47:27; Ezekiel 37:15–28;
Luke 6:17–38

The break between this week's *parasha* and *Miketz* last week occurs at a significant moment. After Joseph's reproach and seemingly just insistence that Benjamin remain behind as a prisoner and slave, the narrative is suspended and one is left in tension as to the response of the brothers. How will they react? Will Benjamin be lost to them? Will this cause the death of their father Jacob?

A Guarantee of Forgiveness

The flow of the story continues here when Judah (*Yehudah*) steps forward and proceeds to utter a heartfelt, self-sacrificial plea on behalf of his youngest brother. A key phrase in Judah's speech is the reason he presents for why he cannot leave Benjamin in Egypt: "*because your servant guaranteed my father that I would serve as surety (arev) for the youth*" (44:32). He is an *arev* (guarantor) for his brother. In a financial context, a guarantor commits his own resources to cover the debt of another. The guarantor assumes personal responsibility for the other. He identifies with the one who owes the debt and stands in his place. Is a chord of redemption resonating here?

Another suspension of biblical narrative is evident in the break between the Hebrew Scriptures (OT; *Tanakh*) and the Apostolic Scriptures (NT; *Brit Chadasha*). Here again, after a catalytic pause, the unfolding story of God's mighty redemption continues. One bearing the scepter of the tribe of Yehudah steps forward as guarantor and makes an outrageous claim that seems to overturn legal justice—a plea of pure grace on behalf of the sinner. He will pay the debt in full, to the shedding of His own innocent blood and the giving of His own life for all the guilty—each of whom he loves like a brother.

In this case, however, it is the Father Himself who offers His own beloved Son as *arev*, guarantor, on behalf of all His children. As a result, we are offered the glorious hope that the full outworking of God's act of redemption will eventuate in an era of true shalom and unity in love. An era that will be ushered in when the same "Lion of the tribe of Judah"—the Messiah of the house of David—will appear as the King of kings and God's Kingdom will be established in all the earth in peace and for blessing.

Don't Quarrel on the Way!

The brothers leave Egypt to return to their father Jacob with wagons laden with food and gifts and the proclamation that "*the good things of all the land of Egypt are yours*" (45:20). They have the assurance of Pharaoh's welcome and protection and the promise of Joseph that he will care and provide for them in order that they not perish in the famine. And yet his parting words to them are, "*Do not quarrel on the way!*" (45:24). Their sin is forgiven, they have the guarantee of all good things, and yet they need to be exhorted not to quarrel on the way! Is this not true of us as Yeshua's brothers and sisters, as children of God? We have been given all we need for the journey, with the assurance of a gloriously bountiful eternity, and yet how easily we fall into the sin of quarreling on the way.

Joseph had a deep and God-given understanding of human nature. He knew that, in spite of their sudden good fortune his brothers would likely indulge in recriminations and blame regarding the past. They would surely experience some trepidation at the prospect of revealing to Jacob that Joseph was not only alive but had risen to a pre-eminent position in Egypt and had, in fact, become their deliverer. Would their guilty secret be revealed? Would they incur the wrath of their father? We discover that in Joseph's full and free forgiveness their sin is truly redeemed and removed "as though it had not happened." It is not referred to again in the Scriptures.

Quarreling and strife are evidence that we are not walking in the peace and blessing the Father commands when His children are *dwelling in unity* (Psalm 133). God always causes the sediment of old, harbored sin to rise to the surface so that we might recognize it, take responsibility for it, and repent of it. When we confess it and release it into the nail-scarred hands of Yeshua, we can rest in the knowledge that we are fully forgiven and cleansed.

We know the promised day will come when all will be made new and:

> *God himself will be with [His people]; he will wipe away every tear from their eyes, and death shall be no more, neither shall there be mourning nor crying nor pain any more, for the former things have passed away.*[1]

We also know that God, by his Holy Spirit, is our comforter in the present. The Good Shepherd is with us on the journey, and He leads us through the everyday tribulations of this life and guides us to *springs of living water.*[2] Our Father can wipe away every tear from our eyes, even now. As His redeemed children let us determine in gratitude to pursue peace, to encourage one another in love and kindness, and not to quarrel along the way!

One in Thy Hand

The prophet Ezekiel preaches powerfully on the themes of repentance and Divine forgiveness, and in this week's *haftarah* he prophesies a glorious message of unity. The children of the "houses" of Joseph and Judah, scattered in all the earth, will be gathered and bound together as one in the House of God. God promises:

> *I will save them out of all their dwelling places where they have sinned, and will cleanse them; so shall they be my people and I will be their God. And my servant David shall be king over them and they shall have one shepherd; they shall also walk in My ordinances and observe My statutes and do them…*
>
> *Moreover, I will make a covenant of peace with them—it shall be an everlasting covenant with them… And the nations shall know that I AM the LORD that sanctifies Israel, when My sanctuary shall be in the midst of them forever.*[3]

It is an immeasurable privilege to be amongst those who even now are "one in His hand" and will be for all eternity.

---

1 Revelation 21:4-5

2 Revelation 7:17

3 Ezekiel 37: 23–28

Va'yechi - ויחי

And He Lived

Genesis 47:28–50:26; 1 Kings 2:1–12;
1 Peter 1:3–13

This week we arrive at the conclusion of *B'reishit*, the first book of the Torah. And so we say, together with all Israel who are studying the *par'shiyot ha'shavua* (the weekly portions): "*Chazak, chazak ve'nitchazek*!" Be strong, be strong, and may we be strengthened in our pursuit of the depths of truth in the precious Word of God.

The *parasha* recounts that Jacob is reaching the end of his earthly journey: *The time drew near that Israel must die* (47:29). He is aware of this and he makes a solemn request of Joseph that he not be buried in Egypt but in the Land promised by God to him and his descendants forever. He specifically designates the place of burial—the cave of Machpelah in Hebron, where Abraham and Sarah, and his parents, Isaac and Rebekah, are buried. Joseph swears to do this and Jacob is satisfied and resigns himself to a peaceful death.

Jacob's Blessings

Although, externally, Jacob had lived an unsettled and storm-tossed life, he was constantly aware of the presence of God with him. As the title *Vayechi* tells us, "And Jacob *lived*." He lived in growing *shalom*—wholeness of being—and now he is prepared to die at peace with God and with man.

This well-earned peace is expressed in prophetic blessing. His first blessing is extended to Joseph's sons Ephraim and Manasseh. This is the first occurrence of the laying on of hands in blessing, and may be the only direct blessing of grandchildren in the Scriptures. In fact Jacob transfers to Joseph a double portion through his sons, each of whom is given equal inheritance with Joseph's brothers (48:5). In so doing he awards Joseph the "rights of the true firstborn."[1]

Jacob's blessing of his sons, the future tribes of Israel, is recorded in chapter 49. The future descendants of his sons remain known as the "children of Israel" in honor of this father of the "household of faith". Now they gather around him to receive his final blessings before his death. Jacob relies on the Lord—*El Shaddai*, God the mighty provider—to reveal a leader who will maintain the strength and unity of the family that is destined to become a holy nation, chosen by and set apart unto his God.

This is the only deathbed scene recorded in the Torah, the significance of which perhaps underscores the anticipation of an important transition and expansion of the covenant with Israel the father to Israel the nation.

The End of Days

Jacob prefaces the individual blessings upon his sons with the words: "*...that I may tell you that which shall befall you in the latter days* (*acharit ha'yamim*)" (49:1). This phrase, as used in the writings of the Prophets, refers to the future Messianic era. An example from the prophetic writings is found in Isaiah 2:2-3, which is echoed in Micah 4:1-2.

> *It shall come to pass in the latter days (acharit hayamim) that the mountain of the house of the* Lord *shall be established as the highest of the mountains; ...and peoples shall flow to it, and many*

> *nations shall come and say: 'Come, let us go up to the mountain of the* Lord, *to the house of the God of Jacob; that He may teach us His ways and we may walk in His paths.' For out of Zion shall go forth the Torah, and the word of the* Lord *from Jerusalem.* [2]

Immediately, Jacob's words of personal blessing take on universal importance. Indeed, Jacob's blessings highlight the Messiah who will be the provider of the bread of life to the nations; the same King who will usher in the end of days and be enthroned on Mount Zion.

It transpires that Jacob's leadership role is divided between Judah and Joseph[3]. Judah, *Yehudah*, is acknowledged as the worthy ancestor of King David, from whom "*the scepter shall not depart*" and "*to Him shall the obedience of the peoples be*" (49:10). And Joseph, *Yosef*, is the one set apart and crowned by God (49:26), the righteous and "*fruitful vine*" (49:22) who will reach out to feed and give life to many nations.

The Anointed One

We see the fulfillment of *Mashiach ben Yosef* (Messiah the son of Joseph) in *Yeshua*—Jesus of Nazareth—through whom the bread of life and the light of the Word have gone forth to the ends of the earth. Now, with all Creation, we eagerly await the sudden glorious appearing of *Mashiach ben David* (Messiah the son of David).

This same Yeshua, slain as the spotless Passover Lamb to bring deliverance to all peoples, to liberate all sinners from bondage, will return in the latter days as the Lion of the tribe of Judah. In that day the remnant of Israel, the whole house of Jacob, will be redeemed, as God's angelic messenger Gabriel promised His mother *Miryam* (Mary):

> *"He [Yeshua] will be great, and will be called the Son of the Most High; and the Lord God will give to Him the throne of his father David, and He will reign over the house of Jacob forever; and of His Kingdom there will be no end".*[4]

Midway through the litany of Jacob's blessings (Simeon and Levi are paired as one, with Joseph given a double portion, so this is exactly halfway) he suddenly proclaims:

> *Li'Yeshuat'kha ki'viti Adonai! "I have waited [in faith and hope and eager anticipation] for Your Salvation, O Lord!" (49:18).*

Could it be that the father of the tribes of Israel glimpsed prophetically not only the wondrous Exodus from Egypt but also the culmination of history, the ultimate redemption and final true and universal Kingdom of peace? He was perhaps granted understanding that in the Savior—the Anointed One to come through the offspring of his sons—God Himself, the Creator of the universe, would be revealed with increasing glory as the Lord of Redemption for all the earth.

Chazak, chazak, ve'nitchazek!
Be strong, be strong, and let us strengthen one another!

---

1 Dr. Rabbi J.H. Hertz, *Pentateuch and Haftorahs*, 180.

2 Further "latter day" / "end of days" references: Deuteronomy 4:29-31, Jeremiah 30:24—31:7, Daniel 10:12-14, Hosea 3:5.

3 The names of Judah and Joseph are often linked in Scripture, e.g. Genesis 46:28, Joshua 18:11, Zechariah 10:6.

4 Luke 1:32-33

EXODUS

SHEMOT - שמות

Exile - Place of Redemption

The Torah narrative has a timeframe although the truths communicated by its Author are timeless. In the words of the renowned Jewish teacher and author, Abraham Joshua Heschel:

> The Bible is not an end but a beginning; a precedent, not a story.
>
> Its being embedded in particular historic situations has not deterred it from being everlasting…
>
> It continues to scatter seeds of justice and compassion, to echo God's cry to the world and to pierce man's armor of callousness[1].

The focal point of this second book of the Torah is the Exodus from Egypt, which happened at a particular time in ancient history and yet, in each generation, the story is ever new. The lessons to be learnt and the meanings to be discovered are vitally real and accessible to each individual soul at the moment of searching. As with every portion of Scripture, the layers of understanding embedded in the text yield rich rewards as often as they are revisited.

When occupied with the study of Torah one soon recognizes that a recurring theme is the connectedness of opposites, such as male and female, day and night, conscious and unconscious, birth and death, slavery and freedom. The one helps define the other. Many of these opposites are dramatically explored in the book of Exodus.

The opposing realities of Exile and Redemption form a central theme that characterizes the book. This is described on different levels, for example: the physical deliverance from bondage to freedom, the illumination of the darkness of the soul, and the powerful infilling by the Spirit of God of empty, meaningless lives lived in separation from God.

On our present journey, at the completion of *B'reishit* (Genesis) and at the start of *Shemot* (Exodus), may we be strengthened in our knowledge and understanding of the precious Word of God. May we also be given strength physically to live what we are learning, in order to draw closer to the Living Word—the Author and Finisher.

---

[1] Abraham Joshua Heschl, *I Asked for Wonder, A Spiritual Anthology*, Edited by Samuel H. Dresner , Crossroad, NY, 1992, 75.

Shemot - שמות

Names

Exodus 1:1–6:1; Isaiah 27:6–28:13, 29:22–23;
Hebrews 11:23–29

Freedom from Bondage

We find the constant exhortation in daily Jewish prayers as well as those of *Shabbat*, and in the traditional recounting of the story of the Exodus at the *Seder* meal on the first night of *Pesach* (Passover): *Remember that you were slaves in Egypt.* This is accompanied by the addendum: *Tell it to your children.* Over and over throughout the centuries the story has been remembered, relived and retold to the children of Israel.

Yet, in the midst of the many words and frequent retellings of the Exodus story, and despite the exuberant annual Passover *Seder*, the heart of the mystery remains hidden. It is too intimate to be laid out openly in black and white on the pages of the historical text, subject to uncaring scrutiny and analytical dissection. Like the Holy of Holies in the Tabernacle, it is enfolded behind sheltering curtains. Perhaps the mystery of God's heart of love is more clearly expressed in the earnest longings and rich, joyful imagery of the Song of Songs; however, it also is to be found at the core of the book of Exodus.

Pesach, the Hebrew name of the Passover Feast commanded by the Lord, can be divided into two words: *peh* and *sach*, which translate as "mouth speaks." In the light of the text of the *parasha*, as well as the book of *Shemot*, this points to the revelation of truth through the Divine Word that issues from the mouth of God, and also to the human ability and freedom to speak. A slave suffers not only the total loss of control over his or her physical life, but also the imprisonment of silence. Slaves have no right to speak, no freedom of expression, no means of sharing their opinions or their hearts. This loss of articulation of 'selfhood' is surely the greatest loss. Only when the bitterly oppressed Israelite slaves lift their voices and cry out does God set His plan of deliverance in motion.

In normal circumstances, one usually experiences deep regret in speaking rashly when one would have been wiser to remain silent. Words indeed have power and their use involves risk. However, much also can be lost in the limiting safety of silence. It is in the tension between self-protective silence and the self-disclosure of speech that each person struggles for authentic freedom before God and with one another. The biblical narrative reveals that it is through the gift of His Word and His Spirit, presented to His people after their physical liberation, that God sets free the imprisoned heart.

A joyful discovery awaits each 'self' that reaches out for meaning in relationship with God: we find that God's hand already is extended in longing to us—eager to woo us with His Word of love and to draw us into His close embrace.

Names and Fire

The name of the second book of the Torah and this week's portion is taken from the first verse's listing of the Hebrew names (*shemot*) of the sons of Israel. As a result of Pharaoh's senseless hatred and persecution (in what, in effect, is the first record of deliberate Anti-Semitism), these descendants of Jacob have lost their identity and become nameless slaves. Then a son is born to one of these lowly enslaved families, whose name will rise as a star in the history of the Jewish people and the nations—Moses, *Moshe.* God will choose this man to lead His people from the exile of Egypt into freedom and redemption.

We read that Moses, after his flight from Egypt into the Midian wilderness, marries Zipporah, the daughter of Jethro the wise Midianite priest, and serves his father-in-law by tending his sheep. Moses leads a settled, contented life.

One particular day, while guiding his flocks to grazing ground, he arrives at the *mountain of God, Horeb* (3:1) and has an encounter that radically changes his lifestyle. He sees a thorn bush burning and pauses to investigate. Moses notices that although it is fully ablaze, the bush is not being consumed.

What fire is this that does not burn and destroy while it radiates flames of light and warmth? He learns that it is the *Shekhinah*, the fire of God's Presence, when God speaks to him from the heart of the flames. He calls Moses to return to Egypt and to demand that Pharaoh let the Israelite people go that they might worship God in the desert. He assures Moses that He will be with him and reveals His Name to him:

> *I AM WHO I AM. And He said, "Say this to the people of Israel, I AM—YHWH—has sent me to you." God also said to Moses, "Say this to the people of Israel, The* Lord, *the God of your fathers, the God of Abraham, the God of Isaac, and the God of Jacob, has sent me to you: this is My Name for ever, and thus I am to be remembered throughout all generations"* (3:14-15).

YHWH (*yod*, *heh*, *vav*, *heh*) is the God who *was* who He was, *is* who He is, and *will be* who He will be. He is the same God of Abraham, Isaac and Jacob—the God of Israel—yesterday, today, and forever.

It is significant that Israel's redemptive process begins at this place—the mountain of God, *Horeb* (Sinai). Moses will lead the children of Jacob to this same place once they are delivered from Egypt, and here God will appear in fire once again. At this mount He will reveal Himself and present His redeemed people with His Word, the Torah—the *Esh Daht,* the fire of revelation of God's perfect will[1]. The Torah is indeed a holy fire, given to penetrate and purify the people of God with truth, and to warm and revive us with its grace.

---

1 Deuteronomy 33:2

Va'era - וארא

And I Appeared

Exodus 6:2–9:35; Ezekiel 28:25–29:21;
Romans 9:14–26

The stage is set for a dramatic confrontation between the God of Israel and the ruler of the then known world—Pharaoh. God warns Moses that Pharaoh's heart is hardened and he will not be willing to hear them. As Avivah Gottlieb Zornberg describes[1] :

> Pharaoh as impassive, enigmatic, represents a certain Egyptian ideal: the Sphinx, inexpressive, above human discourse. He becomes a demonic expression of the human desire to be unchanging and invulnerable, like God.

A battle of wills is imminent but the outcome will demonstrate the extent of God's power above the gods of Egypt, chief of which is Pharaoh himself.

Moses will not face Pharaoh alone. God appoints Aaron to be his spokesman: "*You shall speak all that I command you; and Aaron your brother shall tell Pharaoh to let the people of Israel go out of his land*" (7:2). Moses and Aaron are brothers and of the tribe of Levi, yet each has his individual strengths and weaknesses. We see at the outset of God's redemption of His people a model of partnership, of teamwork, of "going out in twos" as Yeshua commanded His disciples in order to fulfill His commission (Luke 10:1). If we try to stand alone, relying on our own strength, we are bound to seriously limit the work the Lord has purposed to accomplish in and through us.

Moses' Rod

The simple, yet vital, tool of the shepherd in Moses' hand becomes the symbol of God's authority. A carved branch of wood is transformed to bear the miraculous power of the Almighty Creator of the universe. We are told that Moses is the most humble man on earth[2] and he is referred to as "the servant of the Lord" more often than anyone else in the Scriptures. To realize one's call as a partner of God, to work with Him in the establishing and building of His Kingdom, demands a true humility that is the result of a clear understanding of who one is before God. To avoid the dangerous pitfall of arrogance in the face of success, when God's power is demonstrated through one of His servants, there must be a realization that of ourselves we are but "dust and ashes." All goodness, all power, and all honor flow from Him and must return to Him, that His Name be magnified in the earth. He alone is God!

And yet, God calls us to partner with Him in His work of Redemption. No worldly king or ruler would allow lowly servants to wear his robes and crown and use his seal of authority, and most surely would prohibit them from using his name. Yet God our Father willingly imparts His majesty and dignity upon all His subjects. In the Kingdom of God, the King of kings, Yeshua, robes and crowns us with His righteousness and bestows upon us the authority and seal of His Holy Spirit in order that we might be His ambassadors wherever He may send us[3]. In Him all can be raised up from the position of willing slaves to that of esteemed sons and daughters. One is then brought into the Father's house and set to work in the family business!

And the LORD said to Moses, "See, I make you as God to Pharaoh" (7:1). There is commentary in the *Midrash* [4] on this interesting verse, which proposes that one of the reasons Moses, a mere man, was sent to confront Pharaoh was in order that the self-exalted ruler who said: "*The Nile is mine, and I made it*' (Ezekiel 29:9), would be compelled to look upon one born a slave and see the image of God.

Stages of Freedom

God proclaims as a precondition for and the ongoing assurance of freedom: "*I AM YHWH*" (6:6). Once again, as in the opening verse of the *parasha*, He reaffirms the Name revealed to Moses at the burning bush. Previously the patriarchs had known God as *Elohim*—the Almighty, Creator of heaven and earth, to whom all creation bows; the name that describes the ineffable, transcendent nature of His Being, which is far beyond human understanding. Now God discloses, in the name YHWH (*Adonai*, LORD), the One who desires relationship with His children and reaches out in dynamic "face-to-face" revelation of Himself. Dr. J.H. Hertz comments:

> [The revelation of God's Name, *YHWH*] is not intended to inform Moses what God is *called*, but to impress upon him that the guarantee of the Divine promises lay in the nature of the Being who had given the promises. Just as Pharaoh declared, "I am Pharaoh!" (Genesis 61:44) as a declaration of his power and authority, not merely as a pronouncement of his name, so God declares: "I AM *YHWH!*" [5]

Through the process of the plagues God progressively demonstrates His power as Creator over water and land, over animals and people, and over life and death. Ultimately Pharaoh himself, although unwillingly, will also bow to His Name.

The four expressions in chapter 6, verses 6-7, represent the progressive stages of redemption from Egypt and provide the basis for the four cups at the Passover Seder.

Ve'hotzati **- I will bring you out.**

God Himself will do it. The role of the people is one of obedience in following His guidance. We need only to hear and to obey His voice; God does the rest.

Ve'hitzalti **- I will rescue you.**

The Hebrew verb *hitzil* implies rescue from an impending danger. He goes before us to prepare the way, and is our protection and strength in times of trouble.

Ve'ga'alti **- I will redeem you.**

Ga'al denotes redemption from an existing destructive process. The *go'el*, redeemer, steps in on behalf of an indebted or enslaved kinsman to pay the ransom and to gain his release. This role of Kinsman Redeemer is perfectly filled by Yeshua our Messiah.

Ve'lukachti **- I will take you to Myself as a people.**

This is the first statement of Israel's destiny as a people set apart unto God. Their existence is founded upon Him and their destiny inextricably bound up with Him. Israel is His, forever.

God, our Savior Redeemer, has provided the way to escape the bondage of the world, with its unloving, "unhearing," unresponsive gods. In Yeshua, the door is open in loving welcome and all peoples can freely enter the Father's house. In that place all, as sons and daughters, gain the fullness of freedom He always intended for His children.

---

[1] Avivah G. Zornberg, *The Particulars of Rapture, Reflections on Exodus*. 99, 104.

[2] Numbers 12:3

[3] 2 Corinthians 5:20

[4] *Midrash Shemot Rabbah.*

[5] Dr. J.H.Hertz, *Pentateuch and Haftorahs*. 232.

Bo - בא

Come

Exodus 10:1–13:16; Jeremiah 46: 13–28;
Luke 2:22–41

We are familiar with God's command: *Lekh!* Go! in the book of *B'reishit.* Abraham, for example, was told: *Lekh lekha. Go you … to the land that I will show you* (Genesis 12:1). It is a command that calls for the obedience of faith, of which Abraham is an archetype. Now God says to Moses: *Bo!* Come! This is a more reassuring command. He says, in effect, "Come to Me and we will go to Pharaoh together." It emphasizes the fact that God is with him and, in fact, has gone before him to prepare the way. Moses needs simply to join Him and cooperate with the plan already set in place. "*Bo*" is an invitation rather than a command; one that requires a response of trust and loving compliance.

Bo, be'vakasha! Please Come!

The glorious invitation, "Come!" echoes beautifully through the Scriptures. Let us take a moment to examine a few instances:

King David calls to us in the Psalms: *Come, let us worship and bow down, let us kneel before the LORD, our Maker! For He is our God* (95:6-7). And, *Come into His presence with singing. Know that the LORD is God!* (100:3-4).

In the joyful, awesome tenderness of the Song of Songs, the Beloved softly calls to his Bride to come away with Him for the set time has come: *Arise, my love, my fair one, and come away; for lo, the winter is past, the rain is over and gone* (2:13-14).

The resounding promise of God through his prophet Isaiah rings out: *Come now, let us reason together, says the LORD. Though your sins are like scarlet, they shall be as white as snow* (1:18). The invitation is then extended to God's redeemed: *Come, let us go up to the mountain of the LORD, to the house of the God of Jacob; that he may teach us His ways and that we may walk in His paths* (2:3).

How blessed we are to hear the words of God's Anointed Son, Yeshua, the Good Shepherd who became the Lamb of Sacrifice and lay down His life for the sheep: *Come to Me, all who labor [who are enslaved] and are heavy laden, and I will give you rest (shalom)*[1].

He came to set captives free, once and for all. His shed blood on the doorposts of our hearts gives testimony that we can walk from death into life. Just as He cried with a loud voice, "*Lazarus, come forth!*"[2], and vanquished the hold of death, so He calls to each of us, "Come, follow me!"

> *He who testifies to these things says, "Surely I am coming soon"* (Revelation 22:20).

Rosh Chodesh - The Month Begins

Our *parasha* contains an interesting emphasis on the new month, *Aviv* (meaning: Spring) that begins on the eve of the Exodus. *This month shall be for you the beginning of months (rosh chodashim); it shall be the first month of the year for you* (12:2). The Exodus from Egypt marks a fresh beginning in the history of mankind, and Israel is now given a new calendar based on the lunar cycle. Each new moon will mark the start of a new month, *Rosh Chodesh*.

Each *Rosh Chodesh* is considered a *Mo'ed*—an appointed time of meeting with the Lord—when special sacrifices were offered[3], and one enjoyed gathering with family and friends, and meeting with others one usually might not encounter.[4] The literal meaning of the word *mo'ed* is "joining together," a point of connection.

The Hebrew word *chadash* (new) is derived from the same root as *cho'desh* (month), and also *chi'dush* (renewal). Each month the moon passes through a period of darkness. Then it reappears. The first sliver of moon is a sign of its renewal. It gradually increases in size and in its ability to reflect more of the sun's light, until it waxes full and radiant once more. So it is with life. We experience times of fullness, when all is bright and our faith is strong. Then come times of waning, when things seem to contract and diminish; times of suffering, uncertainty, waiting. The moon reminds us that, no matter whether we can see it or not, the sun is always there. The darkness will pass and the light will again shine forth in growing glory.

In the light of Yeshua, we can specifically remember every *Rosh Chodesh* that no matter what dark times we might be experiencing the Son is always there. He imparts His light to us and renews us with His warmth and truth. As we receive His light we can reflect His radiance in the darkness and bear witness to the reality of His Presence and the renewal of life found in Him.

Pesach - Passover

The establishment of the festival of *Pesach* (12:14) interrupts the progression of the plagues that God inflicts upon Egypt. It occurs immediately before the final plague of the death of the first-born of men and cattle. On the tenth day of the month of Aviv, Moses instructs each household to select a special lamb. They are to slaughter it on the fourteenth day, daub its blood on the doorposts of their houses with a bunch of hyssop, and then roast and eat the lamb. It must be fully consumed that night, together with *matzah* (unleavened bread) and *maror* (bitter herbs). Moses indicates that this celebration of freedom and renewal is commanded for all generations:

> *And when your children say to you, "What do you mean by this service?" you shall say, "It is the sacrifice of the LORD's passover, for he passed over the houses of the people of Israel in Egypt, when he slew the Egyptians but spared our houses"* (12:26-27).

When the plague of death strikes in the middle of the night, the outcry is so great that Pharaoh frantically summons Moses and Aaron. He tells them to leave immediately with their people and all their flocks and belongings. Many others choose to join the Israelites as they flee Egypt.

This significant night of liberation is the start of the journey into freedom. It heralds release from bondage into a place of ongoing revelation of, and relationship with, the God who is love. Pesach has been commemorated throughout the centuries from generation to generation. We are joyfully able to celebrate Passover in the knowledge that the deliverance from Egypt paved the way for the prophesied "Greater-than-Moses," the One who ultimately will lead all nations from bondage into freedom and revelation.

At Passover, and always, let us celebrate our deliverance from the kingdom of darkness and death and join our voices with the *Song of Moses, the servant of God, and the Song of the Lamb* (Revelation 15:3). Let us rejoice in our freedom, and sing the praises of the King of the Universe as He breaks the power of the enemy. We joyfully anticipate the fullness of time when His glory will be established in the earth, as it is in the heavens, forever and ever. Amen.

---

1 Matthew 11:28

2 John 11:43

3 Numbers 29:4; 1 Chronicles 23:31; Isaiah 66:23

4 1 Samuel 20:5

Beshalach - בשלח

When He Sent

Exodus 13:17–17:16; Judges 4:4–5:31;
John 6:32–63

The Shabbat on which this *parasha* is read is called *Shabbat Shira* (Sabbath of the Song)[1] as it contains the inspiring Song of Moses sung by the Israelites at the edge of Yam Suf (The Sea of Reeds). It is a spontaneous outburst of praise and rejoicing at the faithfulness and mighty power of the God of Israel, evidenced in their deliverance from Pharaoh's army by His miraculous act of redemption.

The Song of Moses

> *Ozi ve'zimrat Yah, ve'yehili le'yeshuah. Zeh Eli ve'anveh'hu.*
>
> *"God is my strength and my song, and is become my salvation. He is my God and I will glorify Him"* (15:2).

The Hebrew word *anveh* has the same root as *naveh*—oasis, peaceful dwelling place. *Targum Onkelos*, the 2000-year-old Aramaic translation of the Bible, reads this verse as:

> *This is my God, and I shall build [become] a temple [a peaceful, dwelling place] for Him.*

Rabbi S.R. Hirsch (1808–1888) presents a most meaningful and all-inclusive interpretation: "This is my God, to Him would I be a habitation." In other words: I shall become His house. Hirsch comments further:

> I shall offer myself to Him as a habitation; all my life and all my being shall become a temple to His glorification—a place in which He will be revealed, for He shapes my fate and my inner life. He is the power that moves me. [2]

This ideal expressed in the Song of Moses gives voice to the desire of God's heart that His people be the Temple of His Presence; that the nation be holy—set apart unto Him—and the individuals be priests in His service. When the only-too-human Israelites fall short of this aspiration God gives detailed instructions for building the physical Tabernacle, the blueprint for the later Temple.

Yeshua speaks of the temple of His Body[3]. He exemplified what it means to be a habitation of God on earth. All His will, heart and life were yielded to the Father. All He did was accomplished in the power of the Holy Spirit and in perfect obedience to the Word of God, which He in-fleshed.

The apostle Paul emphasizes: "*Know you not that your body is the temple of the Holy Spirit, which you have from God, and you are not your own?*"[4] It is an inestimable honor to be chosen of Almighty God to be His dwelling place in the earth. It can be done, as followers of Yeshua, by the power of His Holy Spirit. The more He becomes our strength, the clearer and purer our song of praise will become.

Miracles and Might

As the Israelites hastily move along the miraculous pathway between the surging waters, they suffer "terror, anguish, the knowledge that their lives tremble on the verge." [5] They experience great fear. When they see the wondrous works of God on their behalf, however, they are filled with faith and they rejoice.

At the place on the shore of the sea where fear and joy meet, where they witness the destruction of the enemy and experience the birth of true freedom, the Song of Moses is born in their hearts and pours forth in praise. They are drawn closer in their relationship with God Himself. They can point in clear recognition of His mighty power, and in surprised, exultant knowledge of His great love they can say, "***Zeh** Eli!*" **This** is my God! (15:2).

They have seen, as it were, His Face. It is a personal, intimate recognition of the Other. *Mi Kamocha*? *Who is like You, O God*? (15:11). The bitterness of the past is redeemed and they are drawn to dance and then called to walk in the light of His Divine countenance. In the Song they are raised to a higher place of beauty, hope and destiny. This is encapsulated in the final triumphant line: *Adonai yimlokh le'olam va'ed! The LORD reigns forever and ever!* (15:18). His is an eternal Kingdom. Theirs is an eternal destiny.

Back to Earth!

The newly birthed Israelites now move into the wilderness. The wonder and inspiration of their deliverance soon wanes and the murmuring and complaining begin. During three days of journeying they find no water and they criticize Moses. By means of another miracle Moses makes bitter water sweet. Next they grumble and complain of hunger. God responds by providing quails and *manna*—bread from heaven (16:12-15). They are instructed to gather sufficient manna early each morning to satisfy their need for the day. On the sixth day they are to collect a double portion, to provide enough for the following day. This would be the Sabbath, on which they were to rest and do no work, but set it apart as holy to the Lord—a time of special meeting with Him (16:23).

At the culmination of the parasha they encounter an enemy; one who represents those who would seek the destruction of the people of Israel throughout history—the evil Amalek.

The Amalekites attack the weaker stragglers at the rear of the large Israelite group. God again reveals His sovereign protection, but demonstrates that He requires the partnership of His people. As Moses faithfully keeps his hands raised to Heaven in prayer, with the assistance of Aaron and Hur, Israel prevails in the battle under the leadership of Joshua.

A lesson of great importance is embedded at the core of the Exodus narrative. Newly liberated slaves (and such are all sinners set free by God's grace) in and of themselves are incapable of instantly becoming a fitting habitation for a holy, transcendent God. The Israelites demonstrate that this can be done only in co-operation with the One who is our Redeemer and the Song of our heart. Miracles are not enough. Inner freedom and transformation require constant education, reinforcement, and discipline in walking together in community and in communion with God. But, God knows all this. He is not angered by the ups and downs, the doubts and fears of His chosen. He is waiting at Sinai with the gift and revelation the people of Israel need—His Torah and His Spirit.

---

[1] Shabbat Shira is also traditionally called *Shabbat Ha'Tzipporim* - Sabbath of the Birds. It is customary to put out breadcrumbs etc. to help sustain the birds during this coldest part of the winter.

[2] S.R.Hirsch, *The Pentateuch*, The Judaica Press, Inc., NY, 266.

[3] John 2:20-21

[4] 1 Corinthians 6:18-19

[5] Avivah Gottlieb Zornberg, *The Particulars of Rapture*, Doubleday, 215.

Yitro - יתרו

Jethro

Exodus 18:1–20:23; Isaiah 6:1–7:6, 9:5–7;
1 Peter 2:4–10

The *parasha* opens with the account of the arrival of Jethro, Moses' father-in-law, together with Moses' wife Zipporah and their two sons. It is a happy family reunion. We see that it is also a significant spiritual turning point for Jethro. He has recognized the power of the God of Israel and, as well as his familial connection, he desires to unite his spiritual destiny with that of the Israelites. He has heard of all the wondrous acts of God and he proclaims: "*Now I know that Elohim is greater than all the gods*" (18:11).

He brings a burnt offering and sacrifices before God and "eats bread" with Aaron and the elders of Israel. These are, in effect, the actions of one who makes a commitment to follow the God of Abraham, Isaac and Jacob; to accept the yoke of His Kingdom. We see a parallel with the sacrifices brought by the Israelites to demonstrate their commitment to the Covenant (24:5).

Jethro exhibits his care and concern for the welfare of Moses and the Israelites when he offers wise advice to Moses regarding his governing of the people. He then returns to Midian, no doubt as an ambassador, to share the revelation and teaching he has received of the One true God.

Asseret HaDibrot - The Ten Words

It is seven weeks, or forty-nine days, since the deliverance from Egypt (19:10-15) and at the invitation of God the people are prepared to meet with Him at the holy mountain. In a dramatic display of sound and light the King of the Universe appears. It is a mighty revelation. There is an extended blast of the Divine *shofar*, clouds billow, thunder rolls, lightning flashes and, as tongues of flame shoot forth above those gathered, God speaks! The earth itself shakes and the people tremble in fear. It is the first Pentecost.

The "Ten Words" God spoke have resonated through history and are still accepted as guidelines for life wherever people honor justice and truth. The Hebrew word *davar,* used in this context (20:1) means 'word' rather than 'commandment' as it is translated in English. The Greek term *Decalogue* also translates as ten (*deka*) words (*logoi*).

The first word God speaks is a proclamation: "*Anochi YHWH Eloheicha..., I AM the LORD your God who brought you out of Egypt and the house of slavery*" (20:2). It presents the basis upon which the further statements are made. God declares who He is—the LORD who brought them out of the house of slavery. He has wooed them into deeper relationship with Himself and now, just as a bridegroom does his beloved bride, He presents them with a *ketubah*, a document of marriage—concrete evidence of His love and commitment. He desires to bring Israel into His house of love.

Yoke of the Kingdom

An intrinsic aspect of this relationship between God and His newly formed people, Israel, is the understanding that they are freed from the heavy yoke of slavery in order to receive the light yoke of the Kingdom of God. A yoke is a means of guidance and is fashioned to provide assistance in accomplishing the task one is set to perform. In primitive farming practices, for example, the wooden yoke enables the farmer to keep the ox or donkey on course. Often two or more animals are yoked together to share the load.

We are not created to be yokeless. Every individual is 'yoked' and guided by something. It can be physically enforced—as in slavery, Communism or radical cults—or it is chosen, consciously or unconsciously. One can choose the yoke of the world and be guided in its ways, which are essentially paths of selfishness and sin that enslave. Or one can choose to accept God's offer of freedom that is extended in His Word and enfleshed in Yeshua as the Living Word. In Him, one can receive the yoke of God's Kingship and guidance and walk in His ways of righteousness, peace and joy.

The foundation charter, as it were, of this Kingdom is first presented here at Mount Sinai, in the magnificent Ten Words. They encapsulate the truth, wisdom, guidance and instruction of the complete Word of God and, in essence, define the yoke of His Kingdom. Thus Yeshua, the Incarnation of this Word, could say:

> *"Come to Me, all who labor and are heavy laden, and I will give you rest. Take My yoke upon you, and learn from Me; for I am gentle and lowly in heart, and you will find rest for your souls. For My yoke is easy, and My burden is light"* (Matthew 11:28-30).

Kingdom Actions

Upon the willing acceptance of this yoke of the Kingdom of God, one discovers it is a yoke of unfathomable love. Every word of instruction is for the good and highest well being of the subjects of the King. One realizes that in place of an onerous yoke of slavery one has received a yoke that is the mark of highest honor. It is an expression of a Father's perfect love for His children. It is the gift of the Beloved poured out to His *segulah* (treasured possession).

The result of this bestowal and receiving of love and life is Kingdom action—acts that are directed and governed by the Ten Words. The first five are connected with our relationship with God. We are called to:

1. **Acknowledge the Sovereignty of God.**

2. **Worship Him only, in spirit and in truth.**

That is, in accordance with His Word and not in ways devised and diverted by man. Throughout the Scriptures, idolatry (whether in the form of graven images or anything that replaces the One true God in our lives) is considered an abomination.

3. **Use Kingdom Words.**

All we say should be within the parameter of not using the Name of God vainly or falsely. When we honor His Name in our hearts, none of our words will be in vain (insincere, empty, shallow) or false (untrue, unreal, groundless).

4. **Exercise Kingdom Acts.**

This entails taking control of our time, our days and how we use them. God exhorts us in particular to "*Remember* the Sabbath day" (20:8-11). This is a day devoted uniquely to Him and our actions should demonstrate that. But we need to remember it during the weekdays preceding it in order to prepare for it, and carry the sweet memory of it into the week.

He also invites us to "*Keep* the Sabbath day" (Deuteronomy 5:12). We are to guard and value it as a precious possession, one that can so easily be lost or stolen.

5. **Live Kingdom Family Lives.**
We are exhorted to have godly, loving relationships that are based on grace and respect. The basis of other relationships is the honor and respect we extend our father and mother. To honor means to avoid any act that might offend them or reduce the esteem in which they are held. They were partners with God in one's creation and to honor them is to honor God. To establish a peaceful home in which God and others are blessed is to actively extend the Kingdom of God on earth.

The second set of five Words applies to our connection with the wider society. These commandments are directed to our lives as members of a community. They indicate that every person is viewed as equal in God's eyes. Every facet of his or her being is of great importance to Him. The life, freedom, happiness, marriage, honor, and possessions of each one are all under His watchful gaze. Therefore, every word and action towards each person He has placed in one's path in life is of consequence in His Kingdom.

Holy! Holy! Holy!

If we have any doubt, any wavering of faith, any uncertainty as to the reason for, or the value of, our service in God's Kingdom we need to refer to this week's *haftarah* reading. The prophet Isaiah describes his glorious vision of the Lord enthroned, high and exalted, in His Temple.

The six-winged seraphim flew above Him and called to each other: "*Holy, holy, holy is the Lord of hosts; the whole earth is full of his glory*" (6:3). And the foundations shook, cloud filled the Temple, and the prophet trembled in fear. He is undone in the searing Presence of the Holy One and cries out: "*Woe is me!*

For I am lost; for I am a man of unclean lips, and I dwell in the midst of a people of unclean lips; for my eyes have seen the King, the LORD of hosts!" (6:5).

Isaiah is given assurance that his guilt is removed and his sin is forgiven. In turn, he is sent as a messenger of the LORD to reassure His people: *Feel secure and calm yourself; do not fear…* (7:4). *Immanuel*, God is with us! A child has been born to us, a Son given, and all Kingdom authority has been given to Him. He is *Wonderful, our Counselor, the mighty God, the everlasting Father, the Prince of Peace* (9:6).

By the Father's authority and to His glory, Yeshua is crowned the King of kings, the Lord of lords, and He will reign in Spirit and truth over all the earth. *HalleluYah!*

Mishpatim - משפטים

Judgments

Exodus 21:1–24:18; Jeremiah 34:8–22, 33:25–26;
Matthew 5:43–48

This *parasha* is one of the longest in the Torah. It is also known as *Sefer Ha'Brit*, the Book of the Covenant, as it contains the first clear, detailed set of commandments. There are 23 positive and 30 negative *mitzvot* (commandments or deeds). They are presented as a consequence of the exclusive relationship between God and the people of Israel, who proclaimed in response to God's Kingship: "*We will do and we will hear*" (19:8). They have made a commitment to *do* the will of God, demonstrated in their lives by their choices and actions, and to *hear* His instructions and guidance as defined in His Word, as given through Moses.

The teachings listed here illustrate that the God of Israel is passionate about justice, honesty, and morality. They are a combination of moral imperatives, social standards, civil and criminal laws, and guidelines for worship pleasing to God. The *mishpatim* (judgments; ordinances) also establish the fact that a life lived for God includes every area of one's being. His goodness is extended to every last detail of every individual life. Only in the nurturing light of His truth can a person grow in righteousness and prosper in all aspects of life.

Mountain Tops and Valleys

At the close of the portion we see Moses once again ascending the holy mountain, which is still covered with a thick cloud of God's Presence. He will receive the stone tablets inscribed by the "*finger of God*" (31:18) with the Ten Words—the encapsulation of the Torah of God. We can imagine the intense delight Moses enjoyed for forty days and nights as he basked in the glory of the Presence of God; as he saw Him "face to face" and received further instruction to share with His people.

We too are occasionally enabled to enjoy spiritual "mountain top" encounters—times of refreshing and restoration when we ardently rededicate our lives to our Father God. However, we cannot live our lives on these peaks. The air is too rarefied. We need to walk out our journey in the planes of the valley, in the day-to-day routines of life. The light of revelation and wisdom we receive on the mountain can sustain us as we translate the experience into daily actions. In this way the original "fire" on the mountain can continue to inspire us to reach out and to impart its warmth and illumination in the sphere of the mundane.

Pesach, Shavuot, Sukkot

We find listed, in the flow of the ordinances, the three annual Feasts: the *Shalosh Regalim*, literally the "Three Festivals of Feet [i.e., of walking, of 'going up']" (23:14-19). Adult males were required to make the journey up to Jerusalem three times a year to celebrate these particular Feasts. They were accompanied whenever possible by their wives and children, and they were occasions of great rejoicing and fellowship. We read in Luke 2:41 that Joseph, Mary and Jesus made the Passover pilgrimage regularly. It would be reasonable to assume that they also celebrated the additional two.

Pesach (Passover) falls during Aviv, the first month of the Annual Festival Cycle, and the week of the holiday is referred to as the Feast of Unleavened Bread: "*Seven days you shall eat unleavened bread*" (23:15).

The feast of ***Shavuot*** (literally Weeks)[1] is the celebration of the first wheat harvest, which occurs seven weeks after Pesach. It is also called *Chag Ha'Bikkurim* (the Feast of First-fruits). As it is celebrated on the fiftieth day after the Exodus from Egypt it is known in English as Pentecost. Another name for the Festival is *Zman Matan Torahteinu* (Time of the Giving of our Torah).

A connection is maintained between Passover and Pentecost by counting the forty-nine days of the ***Omer***. This is the time needed for the growth of the wheat crops. The first fruits of the crop are harvested and baked into two loaves of bread, which are waved on the day of the Feast of Shavuot as an offering to the Lord in the Temple[2].

We can make an interesting personal application as we walk through the annual cycle of the Feasts of the Lord. It is a cycle of continuous growth for it is the framework for the building of relationship that needs "slow development, the conscious and unconscious processes that cannot be accelerated."[3] There are no short cuts to a place worth going, and God has planned and set in place each stage of this annual journey.

The stages can be applied spiritually as follows:

1. At Passover a wave offering is made of sheaves of the first fruits of the barley crop. This represents the offering up of ourselves, the redeemed slaves—sinners who are received by the Lord as they are, chaff and all.
2. During the subsequent forty-nine days of the Omer, we observe the gradual growth of the 'new creation' life that is planted within us. We count the days, carefully guarding and nurturing the new life springing forth. The new

life in our spirits needs to be watered regularly and gently with the water of the Word, weeds need to be removed, and predators warded off—just as diligently as the farmers watch the new growing crop of wheat in the fields. until the day of the harvest arrives.

3. At Shavuot, the time of the wheat harvest, the first fruits are gathered, and the grain is ground and lovingly baked into the fragrant loaves. These are lifted up in offering and praise to our God, the Giver of all good things.

4. At Pesach we remember that we are but sinners, saved by grace. It requires our co-operation and effort, however, to harvest the subsequent crop and to bake the bread to offer Him at Shavuot. As we do, we offer a fragrant sacrifice pleasing unto Him—the growth in our lives and the fruit of our labors.

The Feast!

The final Feast is the "Feast of Ingathering" at the end of the agricultural year. This is the Feast of Tabernacles, ***Sukkot*** (booths), when the ultimate harvest of the year is celebrated. It is, in a sense, the combination and culmination of the first two Feasts. One eats meals, meets with family and friends, prays, and sometimes even sleeps in the shaky little booth with its roof of leafy branches, and one remembers that one's life is but a fragile thing. One is totally dependent upon the Almighty, even for one's every breath.

Sukkot is also referred to as *Zman Simchateinu* (Time of our Joy). It is a time of rejoicing, satisfaction and pleasure at the conclusion of a year's work, when the fruit of one's labor is gathered in. "The Feast" is symbolic of a life well lived. The saints, the righteous of God, who look to Him in complete trust are assured that they do not labor in vain for they are blessed of the LORD[4]. One's life is like a crop harvested in its proper time, bringing pleasure and satisfaction to the Lord of the harvest[5].

Sukkot, on the universal level, is also a prophetic celebration of the End of the Age, when God will gather in His final, full harvest. At that ordained time, the culmination of the ages, there will be joy unspeakable at the Wedding Feast of the Lamb, when the Bridegroom brings His Bride into her glorious, eternal habitation[6].

---

1 Exodus 34:22; Numbers 28:26; Deuteronomy 16:10

2 Numbers 28:26

3 Avivah Gottlieb Zornberg, *The Particulars of Rapture*, 285.

4 Isaiah 65:23

5 Job 5:26

6 Revelation 19:7-9

Terumah - תרומה

Heave Offering

Exodus 25:1–27:19; 1 Kings 5:26–6:28;
2 Corinthians 9:7–15

At the conclusion of last week's portion Moses was called once more to ascend to the summit of Sinai to meet with God. No doubt the Israelites, gathered at the base, watched in awe as he disappeared into the cloud and the fire of the glory of God's Presence. What great revelation would Moses now receive from the Almighty on behalf of His newly formed Covenant People? This week's parasha provides the answer—God has a very practical construction project in mind. He gives Moses blueprints and detailed instructions regarding materials, items of furniture and their design. He wants Israel to build Him a home!

> *Exactly as I show you—the pattern of the Tabernacle and the pattern of all its furnishings—so shall you make it* (25:1-9).

God's House

The Tabernacle, in Hebrew, is called the *Mishkan*. This term is translated commonly as Sanctuary and means a dwelling place of the Divine. *And let them make Me a Sanctuary (Mishkan) that I may dwell (sha'khan) among them* (25:8). The Hebrew word for neighbor, *shakhen*, is from the same root, which indicates the close proximity that God desires to enjoy with His people.

Supplies for the construction of the Mishkan are to be given by the people as a free-will gift (*terumah*—uplifted donation/heave offering). *Terumah* is derived from the root *resh-vav-mem*, which connotes "to be exalted and lifted up"—to be set apart for higher purposes. Such are all the donations, tithes, or *terumot* that we give freely and lift up to the Lord, including our hearts and lives. When freely yielded to Him, they are set apart for His higher purposes.

Rabbi Bradley Artson offers an interesting insight regarding this account of the Tabernacle:

> The story of Creation unfolded on *six* days, each of which began: "*And the Lord said...*" The instructions for building the Tabernacle are found in *six* sections, each of which begins, "*The Lord spoke to Moses*".[1]

The seventh section deals with the laws of *Shabbat*, echoing the Creation, when God ceased from His work or 'Sabbathed' on the seventh day. Moses instructed that even the holy work of building God's House must cease on the Sabbath. Rabbi Artson suggests that the building of the Tabernacle marks a second Creation. This concept highlights the importance and significance of the Mishkan. It is more than a portable tent for religious ritual; it is somehow a whole new universe!

The Microcosm of the Mishkan

At the very heart of this microcosmic universe is the Ark of the Covenant. It is the only object in the inner sanctuary of the Tabernacle, the most sacred space called "Holy of Holies." Along with a jar of manna, Aaron's rod that budded with almonds, and the first tablets broken by Moses the Ark houses the second pair of stone tablets inscribed with the Word of God. These tablets represent physical evidence of the Covenant—the *ketubah* (the written wedding contract), as it were, between Israel and the Lord. To this day most Jewish couples keep their decorative and treasured *ketubah* framed and on display in the sanctuary of their bedroom.

God promises to speak to Moses from between the two cherubim on the cover of the Ark, called the Mercy Seat, indicating that this would be the place of His Presence. The cover of the Ark is a solid piece of gold with two cherubim of gold, one on each end, facing each other with their wings reaching out and touching. Jewish commentary offers that the cherubim were a male and a female, representing an incarnational view of marriage—the embrace of heaven and earth, of God and His people, the Bridegroom and Bride. To quote John Eldredge: "God is most fully revealed in the embrace of the Masculine and Feminine hearts." [2] His Presence is most strongly made manifest in the holy unity of covenant love. Little wonder that the prime target of evil and of dysfunctional worldly inclination is this same holy space.

The people had covenanted to hear their God, and here, in the heart of the Mishkan, they can seek His face. Rabbi Moses Nahmanides[3] wrote: "The secret of the Mishkan is that the glory which abode upon Mount Sinai openly, should abide upon it in a concealed manner."

The *Shekhinah* glory was concealed within its courts. The power of God's Presence was veiled and enfolded within its holy boundaries. It was the physical point of contact linking the Divine and mundane realms. It was the means by which the 'fire' of Sinai could be carried with Israel through their ordinary day-to-day lives. The Tabernacle, which moved with Israel through the wilderness, was the tangible evidence of the special Covenant of love between Israel and the God of the Universe. This was later established in the Holy Temple built by King Solomon in Jerusalem.

Yeshua, however, prophesied the destruction of the Second Temple, the glorious structure standing in His time, which He called, "*My Father's house*"[4]. He knew that this Dwelling Place of God was destined to become portable once again. This time, however, it would be a living temple, built not by hands but one that, in the power of God's Holy Spirit, would *grow and upbuild itself in love*[5]. Yeshua Himself would be the chief cornerstone, *in whom the whole structure is joined together and grows into a holy temple in the LORD*[6]. The Cornerstone would be filled with resurrection life and set in place; likewise, this temple would be comprised of living stones, those in whose hearts He, as the Living Word, would find a dwelling place.

A Moving Mishkan

Each one who carries this precious life of Messiah in his or her heart is comparable to a small Tabernacle of His Presence; a place where His life can be found and His voice can be heard. This is both an awesome wonder and a great responsibility. We, individually and in unity with one another, *rightly fitted and joined together* (Ephesians 4:16), are the physical evidence of the covenant He has made, *the new covenant written on the heart* (Jeremiah 31:31-33). The New Covenant was ratified by the shedding of His blood in sacrifice, an atoning death that burst forth in the power of resurrection life and then was sealed for eternity in our hearts by the Holy Spirit.

After the Revelation at Sinai and the establishing of the Covenant, the redeemed people became fit vessels for the Presence of God: "*Indeed, all the earth is Mine, but you shall be to Me a kingdom of priests, a holy nation*" (Exodus 19:5-6). The Mishkan was the visible reminder of this transformation and high calling. Today, God's Word to us in Yeshua is, in effect: "All that the physical Mishkan represented—its beauty, meaning and purpose—are now deposited in you in a mighty, transforming work of My Holy Spirit." To what end? In order that the glory of God's Presence be revealed in the earth, in spirit and truth, and that His love can become a visible, tangible reality. In us and through us; when we work and build with Him. To quote pastor Bill Johnson, "The Lord's Presence within us is a river not a lake! It longs and requires to flow through us."[7]

The singular purpose of God's covenant, displayed in the construction of the Mishkan, was to express His great love for His people and His deep desire to be in intimate, covenant relationship with them. In His Creation of the physical Universe, God fashioned the first humans with the need to love and to be loved, to reflect and be enveloped in the beauty of His Love. His Word is a gift of that Love. His Son is the Incarnation of that Love. His House—from the Mishkan, to the Temple, to His people—is the physical reminder and expression of that Love.

The Mishkan indeed represents a new multifaceted Universe, each facet of which is imbued with rich depths of meaning waiting to be explored and discovered.

---

[1] Rabbi Bradley Shavit Artson, *The Bedside Torah*,134.

[2] John Eldredge, author of *The Sacred Romance* (coauthored with Brent Curtis), *Wild at Heart*, and *Captivating* (coauthored with his wife, Stasi Eldredge), Nelson Books.

[3] Rabbi Moses Nahmanides, also known by the acronym *Ramban*, (1194-1270; France and Israel).

[4] Luke 2:49

[5] Ephesians 4:16

[6] Ephesians 2:21

[7] Bill Johnson, *Dreaming With God*, Destiny Image Publishers, Inc., 2006.

Tetzaveh - תצוה

You Shall Command

Exodus 27:20–30:10; Ezekiel 43:10–27;
Hebrews 9:6–14

This is the only portion in the book of *Shemot* in which the name of Moses is not mentioned, although he is still central to the action. The primary focus now shifts to his brother, Aaron, whom God appoints as the High Priest (*Kohen Gadol*). Aaron and his sons are to be instituted and anointed to serve as *kohanim* before God in the *Mishkan*, the Holy Tabernacle of His Presence. Moses is irrefutably the esteemed leader of the people as well as God's prophet and teacher of *Torah* (God's Word and Instruction). Now Aaron is awarded the place of intermediary between God and His people in the procedures of worship and service to God in the Mishkan.

Torah and Temple

Some commentaries suggest that Aaron's appointment caused Moses concern, not as a result of sibling rivalry and jealousy but due to a fear that the worlds of Torah (teaching and studying God's Word) and the Temple (worship and service to God) would be separated. If they were split apart the people might lose sight of the importance of the essential unity and connection between the two. The beauty and splendor of the priestly garments, the interior of the Holy Place, even the exterior beauty of the *Beit HaMikdash* (literally the Holy House), and the ritual activities of sacrifice and prayer might distract the people from seeking and hearing the voice of God. In other words, the glory of the Temple might obscure the truth of the Torah.

History records that by Yeshua's time, during the Second Temple period, this is precisely what happened. The chief priests, who comprised the leadership, were corrupted by the power of their position and their collusion with Rome. The external was what mattered and their hearts were far from God. Then the Torah Incarnate walked into their midst. The light of the eternal Word broke into their religious murkiness. To some it brought comfort and life. To others, when the status quo of their self-appointed kingdom was suddenly threatened, it brought confusion and then rage.

In the life, death and resurrection of Yeshua we see all the separated, dissonant parts of the Torah and Temple drawn together in a glorious, harmonious whole. Mercy and majesty, humility and glory, service and truth merge together in Him. The Messiah, foreseen by Abraham, Moses, King David, and the prophets, perfectly unites the physical and spiritual worlds, the human and the Divine.

As a humble prophet like Moses, Yeshua spoke and lived the Torah of God, but He also was the exalted High Priest who bore His own blood of sacrifice to the Mercy Seat of God's Presence in the Holy of Holies. In so doing, He gained Atonement for sin once and for all. It is a deep comfort to know that this same High Priest is now seated *li-yamin ha'Gevurah*, in the place of power at the right hand of the Father, constantly interceding on our behalf[1].

Garments of Glory

The subject of clothing is a prominent theme throughout the Bible. God Himself fashioned the first garments as an act of kindness toward the naked Adam and Eve[2]. In the closing chapters of the book of Revelation, we read of the shining, white wedding gown of the Bride of the Lamb, made of fine linen[3].

In this week's parasha the priestly garments are described. We understand their importance when God instructs that they be made by those who are *wise in heart, whom I have filled with the spirit of wisdom* (28:3). These God-ordained garments carry a power and meaning that require conscious and intentional fashioning. They are described as raiment *for glory and beauty* (28:2).

Avivah Zornberg writes:

> They represent the grandeur of God, in serving whom the priests too become glorious… The High Priest is arrayed like God's ministering angels… [like] a being so irradiated with an awareness of God that even its vestments dazzle.[4]

She quotes the Ramban[5] as saying:

> The High Priest should be dignified and glorious in dignified and glorious garments, as the text says, 'Like a bridegroom adorned with glory' (Isaiah 61:10).

We see a reflection of these garments in Ashkenazi[6] synagogues today. In the sanctuary the Holy Ark is set towards the east, facing Jerusalem. It is closed and shielded, as was the Holy of Holies, by a beautiful curtain. On Mondays, Thursdays and Shabbat, the curtain is drawn aside and a Torah scroll is removed to facilitate the reading of the weekly portion.

Each scroll is dressed in a special, embroidered and decorated robe. It has an ornate silver breastplate and is crowned with silver[7] crowns of intricate design, some shaped like pomegranates and some with little tinkling bells, corresponding to those on the hem of the High Priest's robe.

The Torah is lifted up for all to see and is then carried through the congregation so that each person may lovingly reach out and touch it with a kiss of their fingers. Men often touch it with the cords of their *tzitzit* (tassels on the corners of their *tallit*—prayer shawl), in recognition of the very reason they wear *tzitzit*—to carry on their garments a visual reminder of the Word of God and of the Author's daily, faithful Presence.

The Torah scroll, resplendently robed and crowned, is also a beautiful visual reminder of the Living Torah, our High Priest and King, Yeshua. May He be lifted up in our lives so that His beauty, wisdom and glory may be seen, and may many be drawn to His life-giving, healing presence.

Ezekiel's Temple

The *haftarah* this week contains the thought-provoking verse:

> *And you, son of man, describe (hagged*—tell, explain) *to the house of Israel the temple and its appearance and plan, that they may be ashamed of their iniquities*" (Ezekiel 43:10).

There is something in the very design of the Temple that can turn hearts to repentance. Verse 11 continues: *And if they are ashamed of all that they have done, portray (ho'da*—make known the intimate details) *the temple, its arrangement, its exits and its entrances, and its whole form.* To those who repent, the deeper meanings will be revealed. It appears that every detail contains seeds of truth that are able to teach the people of God more about Him and how to walk in His ways of loving relationship with Him and with one another. These precious, embedded truths illustrate and communicate what it means to *be* a temple of God—to have God Himself living in your heart and your home.

A beautiful prayer in the Jewish Prayer Book, the *Siddur*, is entitled: *Yah Eli (Yah* is my God). It is read after the haftarah reading on Festival days and contains a paragraph that poetically describes the connection between the Tabernacle and the heart:

> The Lord of Hosts, with abundant miracles He connected His entire Tabernacle; in the paths of the heart may it blossom. The Rock, His work is perfect! Eternally will I praise You saying, 'Praiseworthy are those who dwell in Your house'.

The Sages of Israel state that seven things were contemplated by God before Creation:

> Torah, Repentance, the Garden of Eden and *Gehinnom*, the Throne of Glory, the Holy Temple, and Messiah's identity.

These themes are woven together in amazing and intricate patterns in God's Word and throughout mankind's history. Rabbi Yisrael Ariel, founder of the Temple Institute in Jerusalem, comments:

> The Messiah seals this entire design by bringing each preceding step to fruition. He is the Master-teacher of Torah. He will establish the Kingdom of God on earth, and bring about the collective repentance of man. He will rule over all the earth and mete out reward and punishment—a restoration of *Gan Eden* for the righteous and *Gehinnom* for the wicked. Under Messiah's leadership, Jerusalem will be re-instated as the spiritual capital of the world, with the Temple at its heart.[8]

"*Blessed is He who comes in the Name of the Lord!*" Even so, come Messiah Yeshua and take up your holy throne in our hearts in anticipation of your future Throne of Glory in Jerusalem.

[1] Hebrews 7:25-26; 8:1

[2] Genesis 3:21

[3] Revelation 19:7-8

[4] Avivah Gottlieb Zornberg, *The Particulars of Rapture*, 364.

[5] Ramban - Rabbi Moses Nahmanides, (1194-1270, Spain, Israel).

[6] There are many community groups in Judaism, each with their own traditions, music, styles of dress and culinary dishes. In modern Orthodoxy there are the two broad groups of Ashkenazi Jews from the West and Sephardic Jews from Middle Eastern countries—but the Hebrew Torah is common to all.

[7] Silver represents redemption and rejoicing, e.g., the silver trumpets, Numbers 10:9-10.

[8] Rabbi Yisrael Ariel, *The Odyssey of the Third Temple*, G. Israel Publications and Productions Ltd, 11.

Ki Tissa - כי תשא

When You Take

Exodus 30:11—34:35; 1 Kings 18:1-39;
1 Corinthians 8:1-6

The primary focus of this week's *parasha* is *Shabbat*, the Sabbath. The central and most dramatic feature of the narrative, however, is the idolatrous worship of the Golden Calf.

Ki Tissa is positioned between two portions that render detailed accounts of the Tabernacle. The sequence delineated echoes the pattern of the entire book of *Shemot*:

> Tabernacle — Shabbat — Sin of Golden Calf — Shabbat — Tabernacle.

The very people God redeemed and saved out of Egypt chose to cut themselves off from Him through idolatry in the Sin of the Golden Calf. In the pattern of His Word, however, we see that the Lord provides a two-fold way of repentance and return. One is the Sanctuary of His Dwelling (the *Mishkan* or Tabernacle) and its system of sacrifices and the services of the priests. The other is the Sabbath, a time when the people themselves, as a kingdom of priests, also serve God in a special way in the "small sanctuaries" of their homes. Again we see an illustration of the vital connection between the Temple and the heart; the community and the individual.

Be Still and Know

In the pattern noted above another concept is highlighted—the connection between "holy place" and "holy time". Both are obviously of great importance, but God emphasizes that Shabbat takes precedence over the Sanctuary. This special day is the first thing He calls *holy*. The "Sanctuary in Time"[1] that we are to build takes priority over the construction of the physical Temple. God Himself sets the example, as we see at the time of the Creation: *And God blessed the seventh day and made it holy, because on it He ceased from all the work of creating that He had done* (Genesis 2:3).

Thus, the Israelites were commanded to stop work on the Tabernacle in order to rest and to set apart the Sabbath unto the Lord. Our Maker knows that we need a set time in the weekly cycle to cease from our regular work—even when it is holy work—and turn our eyes fully toward the Source of it all. We need to make time in our regular busy routines, as good as they may be, in order to become quiet and reflect and remember *why* we are building and working, and for Whom.

God says: "*Be still and know that I Am God!*" (Psalm 46:10). We need to "still" our busy minds and restless hearts and rest in His Presence. When we meet with Him at these appointed times in the rest and peace of the Lord of the Sabbath, Yeshua, we come to know our Father God with ever-increasing intimacy. Then we are enabled all the more to see and to savor His Presence in our lives.

The Holy Half-Shekel Offering

The portion begins with details of the special offering to be made at the time of a census, or counting, of the people. The same amount is to be paid by each person, *those twenty years or more* (30:14), whether rich or poor. It is paid as *a ransom [or atonement] for his life* (30:12). This is a powerful illustration of the fact that, in God's eyes, every life is of equal value and every contribution a person makes is of equal worth. No one person can accomplish God's work on his own. Our individual efforts are only fragments, which need to be combined with the efforts of others to produce a complete 'whole'.

At the start of chapter 31, we read that God chooses the extremely talented *Betzalel*, whose name means "in the shadow of God," and inspires him with the artistic designs for the structure and furniture of the Tabernacle. He was filled *with the Spirit of God, with skill, ability and knowledge in all kinds of crafts* (31: 3). Betzalel, however, cannot accomplish his assigned task alone and God says: "*I have appointed Oholiav* [meaning tent or dwelling place of my father] *to help him*" (31:6).

Moreover, God declares that He has imparted skill to *all* the craftsmen who will be working as a team in the making of the many different pieces for the Mishkan and in its construction. Clearly, we need His anointing and we need one another in order to do the work the Lord has prepared for us to do. This fact encourages us to work side by side, each one appreciating, encouraging, and offering help when possible, to the other. Thus the task will be accomplished, for the sake of the Name of the Lord and for His ultimate glory.

The Glory of God

At the Sin of the Golden Calf, God withdraws His Presence and threatens to destroy this *stiff-necked* people who *turned aside quickly out of the way which I commanded them* (32:8). The faithful Moses intercedes on Israel's behalf. He implores God to remember His promise to Abraham, Isaac and Jacob that their children would become a great nation. He points out that the only factor that distinguishes God's people from all the other peoples in the earth is the fact that His Presence goes with them. God relents at Moses' plea and we see illustrated the truth of James' statement: *The effective, fervent prayer of a righteous man avails much* (5:16).

Moses then asks God to show him His glory (33:18). *Adonai*, the Lord, responds that there is one vantage point from which Moses can safely view His glory and His goodness and that is to "*stand upon the rock*" (33:21) next to Him. The Lord hides Moses in a cleft of the rock and covers him with His hand until He passes by. Then Moses glimpses His glory from behind—for God had said, "*... no one may see Me [in the fullness of My glory] and live*" (33:20).

Can we, like Moses, see the wonder of God's revealed glory? Yes! We have the vantage point when we "stand" on the Rock of our salvation. Yeshua said that He first would be lifted up and then He would draw all who follow Him in faith to Himself, to be seated with Him in heavenly places in the glory of God's Presence[2]. When we attempt to stand in our own flesh and strength we falter and fall. but sheltered in Messiah we are considered worthy to see the wondrous goodness of God and to glimpse His radiant glory. In the power of the Holy Spirit we are enabled to stand strong and to view all things from the Father's heavenly and eternal perspective.

---

[1] A memorable phrase by Abraham Joshua Heschel in his beautiful work, *The Sabbath*. Also recommended is his book, *Israel, Echo of Eternity*, a collection of short pieces, which I believe echoes the heart of God for Israel.

[2] Ephesians 2:4-7

Vayak'hel - ויקהל

And He Assembled

Exodus 35:1–38:20; 1 Kings 7: 40–50;
2 Corinthians 9:6–11

The name of each weekly *parasha* is most often found in the opening verse of the reading and provides a key to the focus and meaning of the portion. This week the name is *Vayak'hel*, the first word of the verse in the Hebrew text. The direct English translation is: "And (Moses) assembled (or gathered)…".

The three letter root of the Hebrew word is *kuf–heh–lamed* (k,h,l), from which the word *kahal* is derived. The *kahal*, meaning assembly, congregation or gathering, is a central emphasis of the portion.

The calling of an assembly is usually for an important purpose, and this was no exception. The Lord had given Moses specific words of instruction for the people. They were all, no doubt, aware of the great significance of the occasion and must have gathered with the intent to pay very close attention.

An Offering to the Lord

The subject of the instruction given to Moses, outlined in the next few chapters, is the construction of the *Mishkan* (Tabernacle), which includes details of the materials needed. The Mishkan was the forerunner of the *Mikdash* (the Holy Temple) that would be built in the place the Lord had chosen to place His Name forever—*Yerushalayim*, Jerusalem. The Tabernacle in the wilderness would set God's pattern for the priestly service and the future design of the glorious Temples of Solomon and Herod, as well as for synagogues, cathedrals and churches, and even for our homes as small sanctuaries. We may thus derive from the Tabernacle and its service a pattern for our lives as priests in God's Kingdom and as "living stones" in the corporate "temple" of the body of believers.

Before addressing this vital subject, however, Moses first reiterates the importance of keeping the seventh day as *a holy Sabbath of solemn rest to the Lord* (35:2-3). It is obviously a "life and death" matter in the Lord's eyes and he cautions them, once again, that in their zeal for building the holy sanctuary of the Lord they must remember the day that is holy to the Lord—the *Shabbat*.

The collection of materials was undertaken before building could commence. Moses gave the people of Israel the opportunity to contribute whatever possible in goods and service as an offering to the Lord. He lists the variety of materials needed, from precious metals and wood to fabrics, oil and spices. He also describes the various items that were to be made. There was indeed occasion for everyone to offer something, whether materials or a skill. All that was needed was a *willing and generous heart* (35:22). We can imagine that Moses waited with anticipation to see how they would react. How do we react to a call from the Lord? Do we respond with willing and generous hearts?

More than Enough!

It is a great blessing for anyone collecting funds for a worthy cause to be able to say, "*Dai!* Enough! We have more than enough. Tell the people to stop giving already!" That doesn't often happen, but it did there in the wilderness. This was no half-hearted giving. How Moses, and the Lord, must have smiled in delight.

This act of giving was an opportunity for God's people to make restitution for the sin of the Golden Calf. They could now actively redeem their betrayal of the relationship of love, and their fickleness toward the covenant they had entered into at Mount Sinai. Idolatry is akin to adultery. This outpouring of their hearts in giving all they could in effect restored the *Shekhinah*, the Holy Presence of God, into their midst.

God, the Bridegroom, desired a house where He could meet with His Bride, Israel. But, without the glory and holiness of the Shekhinah residing within, the building would be a façade; an empty, hollow shell.

A Witness of Covenant Love

The Mishkan is also called "Tabernacle of Witness" as it bore witness that the Presence of God was dwelling with Israel. When the Tabernacle and the Temples were standing, this Presence was so palpable that it overshadowed the need for the people themselves to be witnesses. God's desire, however, has always been for His people to be a "living temple"—a loving community, an assembly, a *kahal* – that would be a witness to His Presence in the earth, and also to the fact that the imprint of His holiness dwells in their innermost hearts. The external is not the issue. In the beauty of His Presence, a shack becomes a palace.

The spirit of man is the lamp of the Lord, revealing all his innermost parts (Proverbs 20:27). It is also written, in Proverbs 6:23, *...the commandment is a lamp and Torah is a light.* We witness to the character and presence of the real and true God when we live according to His will and walk in the light of His Word. The more we fill our hearts and minds with God's Word, the more we are able to "be a light" and reflect the truth of His life, His Spirit of holiness, His Presence of love into the world. The more we are able, then, to be His witnesses.

> *Yeshua the Messiah…is the cornerstone, in whom the whole structure, being joined together, grows into a holy temple in the Lord. In Him you also are being built together into a dwelling place for God, by the Spirit* (Ephesians 2:22).

Pekudei - פקודי

Accounts

Exodus 38:21–40:38; 1 Kings 7:51–8:21;
1 Corinthians 6:14–7:1

The Hebrew word *pekudei* means accounts or inventory. In modern Hebrew, a *pakid* is a clerk in an office or a teller in a bank.

A striking feature in these closing chapters of Exodus is the close attention to detail. We are given the strong impression that details are important to God! We see, not only the intricate detailed design of the Tabernacle, its furnishings and the priestly garments, but also the careful recording of the particulars of all the materials that were collected and how they were put to use. This is a clear example of good stewardship, and an encouragement for us to deal responsibly with all that the Lord gives into our hands. *All* we have is from Him—our 'things', our finances, our talents, our work and service—in fact our very life, for which we will need to give an account when we return it to Him.

Yeshua illustrated this principle very clearly in His parable of the "talents"[1]. We read of the master that: *...he settled accounts!* May we be faithful, responsible servants, who can offer much increase to our just and loving Master on His return. In order to do so, we need to keep a regular and careful inventory of our lives and deeds—and keep a watchful eye on the details.

Garments of Light

Throughout the parasha, including the description of the special garments to be worn when the priests ministered in the Holy Place, the predominant colors are blue (*tekhelet*), purple (*argaman*), scarlet/red (*tola'at shanni*), along with gold, the white of fine linen, and precious stones. Related to themes in the Bible we most often associate certain colors with specific characteristics of God. For example:

- gold – represents divinity; God's presence and glory
- white – purity
- blue – grace and righteousness
- purple – royalty
- scarlet – redemptive life

The science of physics has discovered an interesting connection between colors and light. We need light in order to see objects and their colors. Scientists have determined that light itself is made up of many colors (the spectrum). Our eye perceives color in a complex fashion based on the various combinations of colors of light that strike it. All the colors combined produce white light. The color we see is determined entirely by which colors an object absorbs and which are reflected. If substance did not absorb certain color rays and reflect others then everything would be white. For instance, the eye perceives the color gold when the material absorbs blue light and all the other colors are reflected. [2]

A fascinating application to be made is that the value and beauty of gold represent the Divine, and 'gold' is material that has absorbed and is filled with 'blue'—grace and righteousness. Our heavenly Father, as we see demonstrated in the life of His Son Yeshua, is filled with grace and righteousness, love and truth, and His Divine glory shines forth as gold. Conversely, if blue is reflected when gold is absorbed, we can make the application that when the glory of the Divine (the Holy Spirit) fills something then the fullness of grace and righteousness are reflected—also demonstrated perfectly in Yeshua.[3]

This is our challenge and opportunity as children of God, in Messiah Yeshua. We have received the gift of the Holy Spirit, who indwells us. We have been given the gift of the Divine, the holy—absorbed the gold, His light and life, within us—in order that we may be transformed more and more into His image. As we grow and are refined, from glory to glory, the more we will reflect the 'blue', the *tekhelet*, of His grace and righteousness.

As God Commands, We Do

Great depth of beauty and meaning is woven into God's intricate design of the Sanctuary, of which is said: *And the children of Israel did according to all that the Lord had commanded Moshe; so they did* (39:32b; 42, 43). And *Moshe blessed them.*

It is recorded at the end of the book, when all the various parts of the Tabernacle and the priests and their garments had been anointed with the special oil:

> *So Moshe finished the work. Then the cloud covered the tabernacle of meeting, and the glory of the* Lord *filled the tabernacle* (40:34).

The final blessing is recorded in verse 38, the last verse of the book: His Presence, made evident by the cloud by day and fire by night, *remained with the house of Israel, throughout all their journeys.*

Obedience to God's will brings blessing. As we press on to finish our work, faithfully and willingly, according to our Master's commands, may His glory fill our living temples and may we walk and rest in the light of His Presence, which accompanies us all our days. Now and forever. Amen.

Chazak, chazak, ve'nitchazek!
Be strong, be strong, and let us strengthen one another!

---

[1] Matthew 25:14-30

[2] For more information see www.tekhelet.co.il/tidbit14.htm

[3] A note to those readers who are inclined towards chemistry and science: if you apply this concept to the elements in the Tabernacle there are interesting discoveries to be made!

LEVITICUS
VAYIKRA – ויקרא

The Tabernacle - Place of Connection

We are on the threshold of the challenging and exciting book of Leviticus / *Vayikra*—"And He called". God calls His people into the wonderful light of His Kingdom, and in so doing, calls us to be *kohanim* (priests) in that Kingdom.

The book addresses components of this calling through the example of the Levitical priesthood. The Levites served in the holy precincts of the first dwelling place of God constructed by man on earth—the Tabernacle in the wilderness. The Tabernacle was also the blueprint for the future Holy Temple in Jerusalem and was assembled according to God's explicit instructions as given to Moses.

The light of His Presence and Word of truth is represented in the Tabernacle by the *menorah*—the solid gold, seven-branched lamp-stand. The seven flames of the menorah reflect the seven Hebrew words of the prophet Zechariah, translated into English:

> *"Not by might, nor by power, but by My Spirit," says the Lord* (4:6).

In His Presence, Word and Spirit we find our illumination, our guidance and our strength.

The Reverend F. J. Dake, of Dake's Bible fame, offers these beautiful observations on the Word of God:

> Read it to be wise, believe it to be safe, and practice it to be holy.
>
> It contains light to direct you, food to support you and comfort to cheer you...
>
> It should fill your memory, rule your heart, and guide your feet in righteousness and true holiness.

And in the words of Abraham Joshua Heschl, described in *I Asked for Wonder*:

> The Bible is holiness in words.
>
> He who seeks an answer to the most pressing question, what is living? will find an answer in the Bible: man's destiny is to be a partner rather than a master.
>
> There is a task, a law, a way: the task is redemption, the law, to do justice, to love mercy, and the way is the secret of being human and holy.
>
> The Bible offers us our only hope: History is a circuitous way for the steps of the Messiah.

Vayikra - ויקרא
And He Called

Leviticus 1:1–5:267; Isaiah 43:21–44:23;
Hebrews10:5–25

Vayikra is the shortest of the five books of the Torah and is the capstone set between *B'reishit* (Genesis) and *Shemot* (Exodus) on the one hand and *B'midbar* (Numbers) and *Devarim* (Deuteronomy) on the other. It is poised between the revelation at Sinai, which culminates in the completion of the Tabernacle, and the subsequent wanderings in the wilderness.

The original name for the book was *Torat Kohanim*, Teachings for the Priests. The entire book consists of instructions on how to meet the requirements associated with worship and service in the Sanctuary of God. In effect, they illustrate how to live as a "kingdom of priests" and to lead holy lives of service to the Lord, individually and communally.

Traditionally, Orthodox Jewish children, at the age of five, begin their study of Torah with this book. It seems a strange choice. Why not begin at the beginning, with the riveting story of Creation and the Garden? An explanation is given in the Talmud:

> The Holy One, Blessed be He, said, "Since the children are pure and the sacrifices are pure, let the pure come and occupy themselves with things that are pure." (Leviticus Rabbah 7:3)

The concept of purity is central to the themes of laws and sacrifices that are woven throughout the book. The understanding of purity is one of the reasons God gives for His teachings: ... *that you may distinguish between holy and unholy, and between unclean (tamei* – impure) *and clean (tahor* – pure) (10:10).

The priestly ritual described by God for the Temple Sanctuary is the extreme opposite of the chaotic, ecstatic orgy of the senses indulged in at the worship of the Golden Calf. Life on various levels and dimensions is a battle against chaos. God gave His Word to assure us that the holiness and order He calls us to can be achieved. However, we are cautioned that this holiness must be valued and protected. Order cannot co-mingle for long with chaos; there must be separation in some way between the holy and unholy.

God Calls Us Near

This week's portion focuses on the system of sacrificial offering (*korban*). This is not a new idea but a major theme of Scripture, which we see introduced with Cain and Abel. The sacrifice is described as pleasing to God if presented according to His will, as was Abel's. God rejected Cain's offering ... and we know the rest of the story! Instead of the blood of an animal, it was his brother's blood that was spilt on the ground.

An important question arises: "Why does God need sacrifices (*korbanot*) at all?" One answer lies in the Hebrew word itself. *Korban* is derived from the root *karav*, which means to come close or to draw near. In Hebraic understanding, the offering of the korban is in essence an act that allows man to draw close to God. It is intimately connected with repentance, *teshuvah*, which literally means to return—to restore something to its proper place.

The common English understanding of sacrifice implies "giving up something, to one's own detriment," but this is far from the Hebraic meaning. Korban is not a gift given to benefit the needy other, in this case God. This would carry the implication that He is a stern God of vengeance, who needs sacrifice and the blood of innocent animals in order to appease His wrath. To the contrary, we know that He is a God of love, who in grace and mercy is ready at all times to grant new life and a new beginning.

In our human brokenness and sin, it is we who stand in need of an atoning korban. Sacrifice is a way provided by our faithful Father whereby repentance is enacted when sin draws us away. Through this redemptive act, we are enabled to draw close in loving relationship with Him once again. Besides the atoning sacrifices there are many other sacrifices to offer, for example those of thanksgiving and purification. All are opportunities to draw closer to our Creator.

Why Animal Sacrifices?

Created in the image of God, man has a *neshama* (soul) and a level of intelligent reason that animals do not have. When he sins, he turns against his true self– the person God created him to be–and operates on the animal level. This brings death instead of life to his spirit and separates him from God. He is diminished and not in his proper place in the reality of eternity.

When the Temple in Jerusalem was standing, if a person came to his senses and recognized sin in his life he could bring the required animal for sacrifice to the priests. By laying his hands on its head, the transgressor could actively identify with it and realize that the blood spilt should be his own. As the burnt offering (*olah*) was consumed in flames, it was a vivid reminder that all we do outside of God's will is wood, hay and stubble and of no eternal value. Sin offerings were stark reminders that sin and separation from God bring death, but entering His Sanctuary in repentance and drawing close to Him by means of a sacrifice brings life.

If we believe that Yeshua's life, death and resurrection fulfilled the sacrificial institution and its sacrifices, then we can examine the *korbanot* in order to more deeply understand and appreciate the finished work of Messiah on our behalf.

The Heart of the Matter

The actions required in the sacrificial system of the Temple involved time, effort and cost to the individual. This gave him time to consider his actions very carefully, to face any sin, take responsibility for it and take action to deal with it. The principle is this: if one sins, one cannot purify one's heart with words alone; corresponding deeds are necessary. When Yeshua forgave the woman caught in adultery He said: "*Go, and sin no more*" (John 8:11). She was forgiven and free to go but her way of life required change.

Every detail of our lives is important to God. Our thoughts, words and deeds express who we are, and each of these areas employed in our worship and service to God today are reflected in the sacrifices:

> WORDS: the confession of our lips in prayers of repentance and supplication, and in expressions of thanks and praise.
>
> These are reflected in the *todah* (thank) offerings—or meal offerings—of unleavened fine flour, oil, salt and frankincense.
>
> DEEDS: "taking hold" of the sacrifice—receiving the elements of bread and wine that reflect the body and blood of Yeshua offered on our behalf; and the righteous actions of our bodies.
>
> These are reflected in the *chatat* (sin), *asham* (guilt), *olah* (ascent) and the festal *sh'lamim* (peace) offerings of bulls, sheep, goats and birds.

THOUGHTS: the focus of our minds, our attitudes and patterns of thought.

The "inner parts" (fat, liver, diaphragm and kidneys) in biblical writings symbolize thoughts and emotions—one's inner workings, as it were. These were specifically removed, washed, and burnt on the altar separately.

Sins are born of careless thinking and uncontrolled emotions. We need reminding that ungodly thinking and attitudes must be controlled and changed. Our minds need to be cleansed by the washing of the Word, and by *...taking every thought captive to the obedience of Messiah* (2 Corinthians 10:5). In this regard, devoted study of the Word of God is considered the "highest form of worship".[1]

The importance of the korban, then, lies in the restoration of a right relationship between man and God, as well as the rehabilitation of man that results in right relationships between man and man.

God reaching out to man in great *chesed* (loving-kindness) lies at the heart of the issue of sacrifice. Another emphasis is the fact that one person's actions have a significant effect on the wider society. When relationship with God becomes merely religious routine, compartmentalized and separated from personal, social and moral issues, then the Sanctuary becomes a hide-out and a hindrance rather than a place of salvation and reconciliation.

The prophet Hosea laments: "*It was your chesed which I desired, and not your sacrifice, and the knowledge of God more than offerings*" (6:6).

May we hear God's call to draw close and to bring Him the sacrifices of our thoughts, words and deeds. As we grow in intimate knowledge of Him may we also grow closer, in His loving-kindness, to one another.

---

[1] An excellent teaching, "The Highest Form of Worship" by Dr. Dwight A. Pryor is available via the website www.jcstudies.com.

Tzav - צו

Command

Leviticus 6:1–8:36; Jeremiah 7:21–8:3, 9:22-23;
Hebrews 8:1-6

The name of the parasha, *Tzav,* is related to the word *mitzvah,* commandment, and the plural form, *mitzvot,* commandments. Traditionally, God gave 613 commandments in the Torah. Of these, 248 are positive (things to do) and 365 are negative (things not to do). A Talmudic scholar, Simlai, made an interesting observation that the number of mitzvot correspond to the 248 bones and the 365 ligaments of the human body (Makkot 23b)—indicating that one should obey the commandments with all of one's might.

It is physically impossible, however, for one person to obey all 613 commands. Some apply only to priests, others only to men or to women, and some can be obeyed only when living in the Land of Israel. This reminds us that a whole people, working together as one Body, is required to fulfill perfectly the commands and directions of God that bring peace and life. God's work was never intended to be a one-man operation.

Son and Daughter of the Covenant

When Jewish boys reach the age of 13, and girls the age of 12, they celebrate their *Bar Mitzvah* or *Bat Mitzvah* respectively (literally: Son, or Daughter, of the Commandment). The ceremony announces that they have reached the age of personal accountability for their deeds and spiritual growth. The responsibility of parents is to prepare their children to cross over this important threshold. In God-fearing, Torah-observant homes this passage into manhood and womanhood and receiving the "yoke of the Kingdom" is celebrated as a special occasion of great joy and honor.

In modern Hebrew the word *mitzvah* also carries the connotation of good deeds. To "do a mitzvah" is a way of imparting blessing, and one should continually be on the lookout for such an opportunity and hurry to do it. Any mitzvah commanded by God should be done as well and as beautifully as possible, in honor of His Name. Living a life imbued with *Torah*, the teachings of God, and of *mitzvot*, doing what He commands in loving, joyful obedience, is considered in Judaism to be the most rewarding and fulfilling life—a life filled with His blessing. The Talmud records:

> The Holy One, blessed be He, wished to cleanse and give merit to Israel, He therefore gave them a great number of commandments (*mitzvot*) and an infinite Torah, for it is written, "The Lord desires that His righteousness (*tzedakah* —covenant faithfulness) be apparent, therefore He made the Torah great and magnificent.

This centrality of walking in obedience to the Word and commandments continues through the *Brit Chadasha* (New or Renewed Covenant). Yeshua says:

> *If you obey My commands, you will remain in My love, just as I have obeyed my Father's commands and remain in His love… My command is this: Love each other as I have loved you* (John 15:10-12).

Yeshua here condenses all God's commands into one; the one that is the true foundation for them all.

The Eternal Flame

Leviticus 6:12 commands: *...a fire must always burn on the altar, it may not go out.* The preceding verse states, with reference to the altar of sacrifice: *And the priest shall burn wood on it each morning.*

Here is the key to our service of God as a kingdom of priests: our worship should not be random, intermittent events, but continual—"each morning." Our Father God renews the creation each day in His merciful goodness. The light of His presence and grace shines upon us afresh with each sunrise. In response, we can lift our hearts in worship and gratitude and then go forth in His service to do whatever He has called us to do. In so doing, we carry His light with us into the day.

The eternal flame of His love and Presence is kindled afresh each morning so that "*it may not go out.*" Leviticus 6:12 is a command; it is also a promise. The true flame of God's love in Yeshua, deposited in our hearts by the Holy Spirit, cannot go out. We are assured in Song of Songs 8:7, *Great waters cannot douse [this fire of] love.* To enable it to burn strongly and consistently, however, we need to do our part as priests each day. God provides the holy flame. We present the altar of our hearts to receive it, along with the wood of our service.

Service of the Heart

We no longer serve the Lord with sacrifices burnt on the altar at the Temple. The eternal flame is now a spiritual or inner fire. The two most basic properties of fire are: a) the ability to illuminate, and b) the power to burn. The revelation of God is often accompanied by fire (e.g., the burning bush, the pillar of fire, Mount Sinai and Mount Zion). The Torah, God's Word, is also compared to fire: *Are not My Words like fire?*[1] His Word has the inherent power to illuminate the righteous in love or to burn the rebellious in judgment.

Our response to His holy fire is reflected in our love and in our fear (reverent awe) of the Almighty God. These are two necessary elements of our prayer and service. Our love causes us to raise our hearts in joy and enthusiastic worship of our Father and Lord. Our fear/awe prompts us to serve Him as faithful servants in earnest study of His Word, and then in diligently walking it out as His disciples, i.e. disciplined followers. In the light and warmth of His love and truth our hearts are purified and uplifted and we can more effectively serve Him.

The essence of God's love for His people is the revelation of Himself and His ways through the gift of His Word. Through His Word, first carved on stone, then written on parchment, scroll and paper, but particularly inscribed on our hearts, we can continually return and draw near to Him.

Through the ultimate, all encompassing gift of the Living Torah, His Son Yeshua, and the fire of the Holy Spirit poured out in His glorious resurrection life, this knowledge can flow from our hearts like Living Water from the Living Temple to the four corners of the earth —for the Father's glory.

> It is the working out of this internal Torah [Living Word], and the fashioning of a life in response to it, that we have to bring as our 'fire from below' – our uniquely human offering to God.[2]

---

1 Jeremiah 23:29

2 Arthur Green, *Sefat Emet, The Word of Truth*, 158.

Shemini - שְׁמִינִי

Eighth

Leviticus 9:1–11:47; 2 Samuel 6:1–7:17;
Acts 5:1–11

The portion begins: *And it came to pass on the eighth day (yom ha'shemini)…*

The eighth day is always significant in Scripture. God set in place a seven-day cycle at Creation. Six days of creative work were crowned with the seventh day, the Sabbath (*Shabbat*)—the first entity declared by God to be holy.

The completion of seven days symbolizes the conclusion of a phase, and the eighth day represents a new beginning. If we finish well and learn from the previous phase, the eighth day brings us to a higher level of opportunity than that which preceded it. In this way we grow and move forward and upward on our journey through time.

The first 'eighth day' in the life of every Jewish boy is the occasion of his circumcision or *Brit Milah* (Covenant of Circumcision). He is circumcised eight days after birth as a sign of consecration in his flesh. Thereby, he begins the second week of his life as a consecrated member of God's Covenant people.

A New Beginning

This week we read of the dramatic dedication of the Tabernacle. The High Priest, Aaron, and his sons complete seven days of preparation and then arrive at the eighth day of consecration. The priests surrender the independent, individualistic phase of their lives and enter a new and loftier life set apart in service to God and His people.

It was God's will that the whole nation be a kingdom of priests. By their actions, however, the people proved that although physically redeemed from the bonds of Egypt they still were bound by the mentality of slavery. Mental and spiritual redemption, and the consequent transformation of character, take much longer to achieve for they challenge the independent choices of the individual. As we personally respond to the call of God we incur the privilege and corresponding responsibility of serving the King of the Universe, which involves a yielding of our 'free will' to His higher will. This service is a daily, often moment by moment, exercise of choice.

Aaron and his sons are to be role models to their generation, and to all generations, until the arrival on earth of the eternal High Priest and Messiah of God, Yeshua. In Him, by the power of His Holy Spirit, we are enabled continually to grow in consecration to God and to become more fully the people, indeed the priests, He created and redeemed us to be. The decisions to serve and to grow are still ours, but the power of God's Spirit of holiness is at work in us to guide us and to enable us in every righteous choice we make. Our challenge is daily to dedicate the 'temples' of our bodies to the Lord and intentionally choose to bring glory to our Father's Name through our Spirit-led thoughts, words and actions.

Olah and Orlah

The similarity between these two Hebrew words is no coincidence. The ***Olah*** is described in this parasha as one of three consecration offerings made by Aaron. They are the *sin offering* of a he-goat for atonement; the *meal offering* (flour mixed with oil) representing one's service to God in peace and veneration, and the *olah* (literally, the ascent offering) that is totally burnt on the altar.

The *olah* conveyed the most profound expression of a worshiper's desire to present an offering to God in repentance, reverence, gratitude, or expiation. People were not limited as to when they could present an olah offering. In some instances, however, it was required. For example:

- at the purification of a leper (Leviticus 15:15,30)
- at purification after childbirth (Leviticus 12:6-8, and Luke 2:22[1])
- by a Nazarite at the conclusion of his vow (Numbers 6:11ff)
- at the consecration of priests (Exodus 29:15).

Each of these occasions implies the beginning of new life and the passing away of the past life or condition—vividly portrayed in the total consummation of the sacrifice. The olah offering was a fitting means whereby to express one's deepest gratitude to God for new life.

Orlah is the foreskin, which is removed at circumcision. Often in Scripture the injunction is given to *remove the foreskin of your hearts*[2]. Deuteronomy 10:12 reads: *Circumcise the foreskin of your heart, and be no longer stubborn.* This terminology is found in the context of obedience to God and His Word, and describes how in shame at one's sin and through repentance, one is exhorted to return to the Lord in truth, to stand in His justice, and to walk upright in His ways[3].

The *orlah* and the *olah*, therefore, both symbolize total surrender and dedication of oneself in wholehearted obedience and willing service to our God and King.

Strange Fire

The glorious purpose of the dedication of the Tabernacle is to welcome the Presence of the Lord. The people prepare themselves and wait in great anticipation. Moses and Aaron finally emerge from the Sanctuary and bless the assembled people. Then, we are told: *...the Presence of the Lord appeared to all the people* (9:23). Instantly, fire comes forth from His Presence and consumes all that remains on the altar, indicating God's acceptance of their sacrifice. The people are overwhelmed by the glory and power of His Presence. They respond by shouting and falling forward on their faces.

What happens next is totally unexpected and shocking, and sets a powerful precedent for all who serve the Lord. Two of Aaron's sons, Nadav and Avihu, each takes his fire-pan, adds fire and incense, and waves it before the Lord. We can only speculate as to their motive in doing this. We are told, however, that it was *...strange (zarah* - idolatrous*) fire which He had not commanded them* (10:1). There is no doubt in God's immediate response: ...fire came forth from the Lord and consumed them; and they died before the Lord (10:2).

To view their actions in a positive light, we may consider that their hearts and beings were so deeply stirred by the radiance of the glory of the Lord's Presence that they offered themselves wholly to Him in worship, and He accepted them as *olah* sacrifices. The full text reads more negatively, however, and seems rather to be a strong warning against even an appearance of idolatry by those who serve and represent the Almighty God.

The apostle Paul stresses in his epistles the challenge to avoid every form, and even indication, of idolatry. An example:

> *When Messiah who is our life appears, then you also will appear with Him in glory. Put to death therefore what is earthly in you: fornication, impurity, passion, evil desire, and covetousness, which is idolatry* (Colossians 3:4-5).

The account of Aaron's sons is a startling reminder that those who serve the Lord bear a great responsibility to humbly submit their wills to His. We are encouraged to fully and eagerly follow His teaching and commandments in all things, including the order and rituals of service that are pleasing to Him.

The Power of Silence

The book of Leviticus, as with all of Scripture, is concerned with our use of words. The Torah teaches us much about sanctifying what goes forth from our mouths. Words are powerful. This week we see, in Aaron's response at the death of his sons, that silence also is powerful.

Immediately after the shocking demise of his two sons, Moses turns to comfort Aaron with words of wisdom from the Lord: *By those who come near Me I must be regarded as holy; And before all people I must be glorified* (10:3).

This seems to affirm that Nadav and Avihu's actions profaned the holiness of God. Possibly they were too 'familiar' with God, or were trying to glorify themselves before the people. But what is their father Aaron's response to all this? He remains silent (10:3b).

The Bible seldom calls attention to a person's silence. What, then, is the significance of Aaron's silence? It may be an indication that he accepts God's decree without protest. Or perhaps it suggests that there are times when there is more strength to be found in silence than in words.

---

[1] Luke 2:22. Mary presents a pair of doves at the Temple forty days after the birth of Yeshua.

[2] E.g., Jeremiah 4:4.

[3] See Paul's corresponding teaching in Romans 2:25-29.

Tazria - תזריע

Conceived

Leviticus 12:1–13:59; 2 Kings 4:42–5:19;
Matthew 8:1–4

The first subject addressed in this *parasha* is that of a woman who conceives and gives birth. Renowned Jewish poet and Bible commentator, Ibn Ezra (Spain, 1089-1164), states that this issue is highlighted, "...because that is the beginning of life and therefore the start of the *tum'ah* process [restoration of purity]".

For seven days, until her son's *brit milah* (circumcision) she is *tamei* (ritually unclean). Thereafter she begins a thirty-three day cleansing process, which culminates in the presentation of an offering to the priests at the Temple.

The miracle of new life is a cause for celebration, why then should it render a woman *tamei*? One opinion is that the fact of new life in itself is not enough. A person's life is not automatically *tahor* (clean, pure). It only becomes so when it is consecrated to God. Life must be elevated in relationship and service to the Giver of life otherwise it is empty of true, eternal meaning.

Finally, with the offering brought to the Temple and in receiving the blessing from the *kohen*/priest, the mother enters once again into full community fellowship at the Sanctuary. All celebrate and praise God together with her in gratitude for the new life and with eager anticipation for the future.

Forty Days

To emphasize the importance of this forty-day period after birth, it is recorded in the *Brit Chadasha* (New Testament) that Yeshua's mother *Miryam* (Mary) observed it[1]. The period of forty days is of particular significance throughout the Scriptures. It is recognized as a set-apart time for preparation before the start of a specific event. In the life of Yeshua we remember the forty days and nights He spent in the wilderness fasting and being tempted by Satan. This was the crucible of testing He endured before the commencement of His earthly ministry.

We see this concept illustrated from the time of Genesis. Rain fell for forty days and nights after Noah built the Ark and water covered the earth. Moses ascended Mount Sinai and the Israelites waited forty days for his return. They failed the test of waiting, which resulted in the sin of the Golden Calf. It took Moses another forty days of intercession before he received the second set of tablets that documented God's Ten Words. The spies sent into the Promised Land spent forty days scouting around and returned with a majority bad report. It may not be unconnected that the Israelites who believed the negative news consequently spent forty years wandering in the wilderness!

There are "forties" that may be less commonly known. For example: the minimum quantity of water required for a kosher *mikvah* (ritual immersion pool/bath) is forty *seah* (approx. 240 gallons); there are forty days from conception to the formation of the embryo; and the height of the main entrance to the Temple Sanctuary was forty cubits.

There are interesting correlations to be made, especially if one considers that the letter in the Hebrew alphabet with the numerical value of 40 is *mem*, which symbolizes living waters. The above examples of forty are each suffused with the interconnecting concepts of water, life, and the Word of God.

Clean and Unclean?

The portion continues in chapter 13 with a lengthy discussion on afflictions of the skin, clothing and houses and the necessary action to be taken when faced with these conditions. It does not seem to make any sense unless the concepts of *tahor* and *tamei* are understood. The words are usually translated as clean and unclean, or pure and impure. These words inaccurately imply a state of physical cleanliness as opposed to one of dirtiness and repulsion. A better translation is "ritually" pure or impure. When a person was *tamei*, or ritually unclean, they were barred from participating in the Temple services, including the offering of sacrifices, no matter how clean their bodies were. This separation from the Sanctuary resembled a spiritual state of death.

The conditions whereby a person could be proclaimed *tamei* were somehow linked with sin and/or death. For example, if someone touched a dead body they were rendered *tamei* for a day and needed to wash themselves and their clothes before being *tahor* once more. In this case there is no sin involved. Unless, God forbid, they had committed murder.

If a person developed a certain skin affliction or their house had a mold like growth on the walls (not regular disorders, but 'supernatural' growth identified by the *kohen*) they and it were declared *tamei* and cleansing rituals were to be followed. These rituals all served to impress upon God's people the spiritual realities that sin and death are in opposition to life and righteousness. Sin separates us from the life of God's Presence. The profane conflicts with the holy and, like darkness and light, they cannot coexist.

The challenge of walking in the Kingdom of God, which is Life, as opposed to the kingdom of darkness, which is death, is constantly before us as it was then. It is a daunting thought. However, Paul affirms a glorious truth in his letter to the Romans:

> *For, if by the trespass of the one man [Adam] death reigned... how much more will those who receive God's abundant provision of grace and the gift of righteousness reign in life through the [last Adam] Messiah Yeshua...so that just as sin reigned in death, so also grace might reign through righteousness to bring eternal life through Messiah Yeshua* (5:12-21).

Our Father God has provided victory over sin and death through our Lord and Messiah Yeshua. The elements that would render us *tamei* are done away with in Him, and we are born anew through water and the Spirit. Now, as we faithfully live in Him and joyously walk in His ways, nothing can separate us from the love of God.

---

[1] Luke 2:22

Metzora - מצרע

Leper

Leviticus 14:1–15:33; 2 Kings 7:3–20;
Romans 6:19–23

The affliction translated as *leprosy* is not the disease we know by that name today. Hence, a *metzora* is not technically a leper. He, or she, is one who was sent outside the camp (community, town or city) for a set time once they were declared ritually unclean by a *kohen*/priest. Although the condition had a physical manifestation on the skin, we learn that the root cause is a spiritual one. According to ancient Jewish commentary, the primary cause is considered to be the sin of *lashon ha'ra*—slander and gossip, which indicates an arrogant insensitivity to others.

Being alone outside the camp enables the metzora to examine his life and to come to repentance. Once examined, declared healed, and cleansed by a kohen he is able to return to the community after seven days. On the eighth day he brings offerings to the kohen and regains admittance into the Holy Temple – the Sanctuary of God's Presence.

The kohen completes his purification by anointing (first with blood of the guilt offering, then with oil)

- his right ear lobe—indicating his willingness to hear God's Word;
- the thumb of his right hand—indicating submission of his actions to God;
- the big toe of his right foot—indicating the commitment of all his "comings and goings" to the Lord.

Finally the kohen uses the remaining oil to anoint his head, indicating that his mind and whole being are now yielded to God.

We read in Matthew 8:2-4 that Yeshua heals a leper/metzora and sends him to a priest to complete the final ritual. Yeshua Himself prophetically fulfilled the purification process and thus granted healing and forgiveness for sin, but the anointing with the oil of the Holy Spirit was still to come.

Haughty Cedar and Lowly Hyssop

At the time a kohen determined that the metzora was healed, he initiated the purification process. He called for the following items to be brought to him outside the camp: two live, kosher birds, cedar wood, crimson thread, hyssop, and an earthenware vessel of spring water (*ma'yim cha'yim*—living water). The following procedure then took place:

1. One bird was ritually slaughtered over the vessel of water.
2. He took the live bird together with the piece of cedar wood, the crimson thread and the hyssop and dipped them into the blood and water in the bowl.
3. He sprinkled the metzora seven times then set the live bird free.

We are reminded that the number seven indicates the completion and perfection of something; followed by eight: a sparkling new beginning.

The *Midrash* records a wonderful piece of Solomon's wisdom with reference to the purification ceremony:

> Why are the most majestic and the most humble of plants, cedar wood and hyssop, combined in these rites of purification? Because man is stricken with leprosy as a punishment for being haughty and arrogant as a cedar, and when he hum-

bles himself like the lowly hyssop he will ultimately be cured (Ecclesiastes Rabbah 7).

The contrast of the tall, imposing cedar tree and the lowly hyssop shrub is striking. Hyssop grows wild in Israel, even in stony, waterless places. It is available to all as a popular herb, the rich and poor alike. It presents a perfect symbol of humility.

On the eve of the Exodus, hyssop was used to apply the blood of the Passover lamb on the doorposts and lintels of the Israelite homes in Egypt, signaling the victory of life over death. Also, perhaps due to its absorbent quality, it is believed that the 'sponge' Yeshua sipped sour wine from at His crucifixion was a bunch of humble hyssop. Lofty work for a lowly shrub!

The "Metzora Messiah"

An interesting passage in the *Talmud*, based on Isaiah 53:4, lists one of the names of the Messiah as *Mashiach ha'Metzora*[1]. The Sages of Israel saw Messiah as taking our uncleanness, our 'leprosy' upon Himself.

We can rejoice in the fact that our Messiah Yeshua, the King of kings, indeed humbled Himself and took all our afflictions upon Himself:

> *The death He died He died to sin, once for all, but the life He lives He lives to God. So you also must consider yourselves dead to sin and alive to God in Messiah Yeshua* (Romans 6:10-11).

As our *Kohen Gadol* (High Priest), and by the living water of His life, and His blood that was shed, once and for all, He purifies all who repent and anoints them with the oil of the Holy Spirit—*Ruach HaKodesh*.

He then sets them free as a bird to soar to the heavens—to draw near to the Most High God, just as joyful children run to the arms of their loving Father.

---

[1] Sanhedrin 98b.

Acharei Mot - אחרי מות

After the Death

Leviticus 16:1—18:30; Ezekiel 22:1–19;
1 Corinthians 6:9–20

The portion this week offers a clear example of how the name and opening words often establish the tone for content that follows. "*After the death*" refers to the supernatural death of the two sons of Aaron, who drew too near to the Presence of the Lord in a manner He had not prescribed. The text proceeds by describing the *Yom Kippur* (Day of Atonement) rituals of cleansing, self-sacrifice, death and renewal. The account draws us to confront our own mortality and to reflect on the direction and goal of our lives.

The public observance of Yom Kippur takes place at the holiest place in the world on the holiest day of the year, and is conducted by the High Priest, the holy God-appointed man who is anointed for the task. The deaths of Nadav and Avihu are tragic reminders that special precautions need to be taken before entering the Holy Place. How much more so the Holy of Holies! An emphasis therefore is placed upon the role of the priests, in particular the High Priest, and their responsibility in preparing and purifying themselves and the Sanctuary for this awesome occasion.

A passage from the parasha (16: 4ff) comprises the Torah reading for the Yom Kippur morning service in synagogues.

The passage is located in the annual reading cycle exactly six months before and six months after Yom Kippur. This position of centrality indicates that, as the redeemed of God, it is fitting to walk throughout the year in an attitude of repentance and in awareness of our dependence upon the One who is the giver of, the reason for, and the goal of life itself.

One "For the Lord"

Special sacrifices were offered on Yom Kippur. We read that a bullock was sacrificed for the expiation of the sins of Aaron the High Priest and his household. He would place his hands on the animal's head and recite the prayer:

> *I beseech You, O God: I have sinned, rebelled, and transgressed against you,*
> *I and my household;*
> *I beseech You, O God: grant atonement for the sins, and the iniquities and the transgressions which I have committed against you, I and my household.*
> *As it is written in the Torah of your servant, Moses: "For on this day atonement shall be made for you, to purify you from all your sins—before God you shall be purified."*[1]

This was the only day of the year that the High Priest would traverse the heavy, woven curtain that separated the Holy Place from the inner sanctum that housed the Ark of the Covenant. He would first enter with a golden shovel-like utensil, filled with burning coals from the altar, whereupon he burnt a handful of the *ketoret* (special incense). After the sacrifices, he would carry a golden bowl into the Holy of Holies containing blood from the sacrifice. He sprinkled the blood on the Mercy Seat, the cover of the Ark, and on the ground before it. This ritual was gloriously fulfilled by Yeshua:

> *But when Messiah appeared as a High Priest of the good things that have come, then ...He entered once for all into the Holy Place, taking not the blood of goats and calves but His own blood, thus securing an eternal redemption* (Hebrews 9:11).

This was an awe-inspiring part of the Yom Kippur ceremony. If the High Priest, in this case Aaron, did not enter the Holy of Holies in a state of purity, he stood to suffer the same fate as his two sons. It is said that, as a precaution, a cord was tied to one of the High Priest's ankles so that in the event of his death the priests could retrieve his body. His preparation was therefore intense and precise. Throughout the day he washed his hands and feet at the laver ten times and immersed himself in a *mikvah* (ritual bath) five times. The latter was undertaken each time he disrobed his ornate "Golden Garments" worn before the congregation and donned the four simple white garments he wore when entering the Holy of Holies.

As an atonement offering for the people of Israel, two goats were presented and, in addition, a ram as an *olah* – whole burnt offering. When the two goats were brought before him, the High Priest drew lots to see which goat would be "*For the Lord*" and which was to be taken out to the wilderness, "*For Azazel*" (verse 10). The goat for the Lord was sacrificed as a burnt offering on the altar.

A curious detail of the procedure took place as follows:

> It was considered an auspicious sign if the lot marked "For God" came up arbitrarily in the priest's right hand. In order to ensure that the High Priest could not possibly tell one lot from another, he would quickly raise both lots from the box in a sudden fashion. If the lot bearing the inscription "For God" is drawn with his right hand the assistant declares, "My master, the High Priest! Raise up your right hand!"[2]

Interesting parallels can be observed in passages of Scripture that make reference to God's right hand. It is a sign of power and deliverance, of victory over enemies, of judgment. For example, the first mention of the Lord's right hand occurs in the wonderful Song at the Sea, Moses' exultation of praise after the Lord's victory over Pharaoh's army: "*Thy right hand, O LORD, glorious in power; Thy right hand, O LORD, shatters the enemy.*"[3] Also, significantly, in Moses' parting blessing to the people before his death, he begins by saying: "*The LORD came from Sinai... He shone forth... with flaming fire at His right hand.*"[4]

We find many echoes in the Psalms, e.g.:

> *Thou dost stretch out thy hand against the wrath of my enemies, and* ***Thy right hand*** *delivers me* (138:7).

> *Thou hast given me the shield of thy salvation, and* ***Thy right hand*** *supported me, and Thy help made me great* (18:35).

When confronted by the corrupt High Priest as to His Messiahship, Yeshua gave a direct reply:

> *I Am; and you will see the Son of man seated* ***at the right hand*** *of Power, and coming with the clouds of heaven* (Mark 14:62).

After the Resurrection, the apostle Peter is also questioned by the High Priest regarding Yeshua, and he proclaims:

> *God exalted him at* ***His right hand*** *as Leader and Savior, to give repentance to Israel and forgiveness of sins. And we are witnesses to these things, and so is the Holy Spirit whom God has given to those who obey him* (Acts 5:31-32).

At the end of the age, when the Son of man indeed comes with clouds of heaven in His glory, He will sit on His throne of judgment. He will separate all the nations as a shepherd separates the sheep from the goats.

> *...and he will place the sheep* ***at his right hand****, but the goats at the left.*

Then the King will say to those at ***his right hand****, "Come, O blessed of my Father, inherit the kingdom prepared for you from the foundation of the world"* (Matthew 25:31-34).

One Scapegoat

The second goat "for Azazel", which was first named the "Scapegoat" in Tyndale's Bible, 1530, remained standing before the people in the Outer Courtyard of the Temple. In a powerful ceremony the High Priest laid his hands on the scapegoat placing, as it were, the sins of the people upon it. It was then led into the wilderness and, according to historical accounts, pushed over a cliff to die.

The scapegoat is somehow connected to the *se'irim* (goat demons) mentioned in chapter 17, verse 7. These could represent idolatrous practices one is drawn into by the temptations of the world, as well as one's own inclination towards unredeemed behavior. If we humble our 'natural' inclinations (the animal-like aspects of human nature) under the Kingship of God, then He is faithful to lift us up supernaturally and afford us the victory over them.

Just as Yeshua was raised up from the bonds of death by the power of the Almighty God, we are enabled by His Holy Spirit to rise above the tendencies and bent-ness of our old, fallen nature with its inherent inclination toward sin and the death that results. We can then, following after the Shepherd of our souls, walk upright with Him in a relationship of holiness that endures through eternity.

The Father of all therefore exhorts His people in chapter 18:3-4,

You must not do as they do in Egypt, where you used to live, and you must not do as they do in the land of Canaan, where I am bringing you. Do not follow their practices. You must fol-

low My laws and be careful to follow My decrees. I AM the Lord your God.

The reason for this is Life—the newness of redeemed life, here on earth and for eternity.

Blessed are those who hear the Word of God and obey it[5].

For indeed your reward is great in heaven[6].

It is by faith in Yeshua's finished work on our behalf that we can walk in harmony with the Torah of God now written in our hearts by His Spirit. We can, here and now, enjoy and impart the blessing it bestows.

---

1 Leviticus 16:30

2 Rabbi Yisrael Ariel, Translated by Chaim Richman, *The Odyssey of the Third Temple.* G.Israel Publications Ltd, The Temple Institute, Jerusalem, 5753, 51

3 Exodus 15:6

4 Deuteronomy 33:2

5 Luke 11:28

6 Matthew 16:23

Kedoshim - קדושים

Holy

Leviticus 19:1–20:27; Amos 9:7–15;
Romans 13:8–14

This *parasha* is positioned exactly at the center of the book of *Vayikra*/Leviticus. It is, therefore, also the mid-point of the five books of Moses. As the fulcrum on which the Torah balances, one would expect it to highlight the deepest heart of this precious foundation of the Word of God. And indeed it does. This is considered one of the richest and most exalted portions in the Hebrew Scriptures.

It begins with the words: *Kedoshim te'hiyu. "You shall be holy!"* The pronoun here is plural, indicating that it is the people of Israel who shall be holy. This command to be holy can also be read as a promise of holiness: "You *shall* be holy." It is repeated three more times in this parasha (20:7, 8, 26). We can assume it is God's intent that this message be very clear.

What is Holiness?

The portion follows directly after the detailed description of relationships that are pleasing, or not, to the Lord. This indicates that holiness is connected with relationships—with God and with one another.

If we view holiness in the context of relationships it affects our perception of other people. While we do deeply value our close covenantal relationships, which are holy and set apart from our wider relationships, we also are prompted to recognize the latent holiness in every person. We cannot dismiss anyone as worthless or insignificant as every human being is created in the image of God.

Something holy is seen to be different. It is set apart in some way from the ordinary. In rabbinic literature the word ordinary (*chol*), which does not necessarily mean bad, is often used as the opposite of holy (*kadosh*).

God is the One who first made and called things holy, for example: the Shabbat, Jerusalem, His people. As His children we can imitate Him by sanctifying moments and things in our lives. Our *time* is sanctified, or made holy, when we dedicate it to serving our Father God, and to drawing closer to Him. *Things* can be sanctified when they are used in God's service and to honor His Name. We see *people* as holy when we honor the likeness of their Creator that they bear, however well hidden it sometimes may be! This includes recognizing and honoring the image of God in ourselves, to nurture and encourage His holy image to grow in one's innermost being. We will then increasingly reflect His holiness.

Outward Deeds, Inner Sanctity

Chapters 19 and 20 list deeds that are considered outward reflections of holiness. For example, in chapter 19:

Honoring one's parents (v. 3); Staying away from idols and all that would lead one away from God's path (v.4); Caring for the poor and the stranger (v.9); No stealing, lying or unjust dealings (v.11); Proper treatment of neighbors and servants (v.13); Impartial judgments (v.15).

We need to bear in mind, however, that the outward obedience of the commandments of the Lord is not a means to an end. The commandments are not merely things to do in order to "be holy". Ideally, one's adherence to them and the fruit that is produced in so doing will be outward reflections of a deep and loving relationship with the Giver of the commandments. A relationship initiated by our Father-Creator, who has called us and drawn us closer to Himself as a gift of His love. Our acts of obedience are, similarly, gifts of our love in return.

Do the Will of My Father

The full expression of His relational love is found in Yeshua, who said: *If you keep My commandments you will abide in My love, just as I have kept My Father's commandments and abide in His love*[1]. And, *Whoever does the will of My Father in heaven is My brother and sister and mother.*[2]

Yeshua encapsulates all the commandments of His Father when He says: *This is My commandment, that you love one another as I have loved you*[3].

In order to demonstrate love for another, one takes delight in doing what is pleasing to the other. Our words and deeds are thus an expression and demonstration, a necessary out-flowing, of our love.

At the conclusion of the portion we read God's exhortation to Israel before they are brought into the Land of promise. He presents the reason for the way of life to which He calls His people:

> *You must not live according to the customs of the nations I am going to drive out before you. Because they did all these things [not in accord with the Word of God] I abhorred them… I am the Lord your God who has set you apart from the nations. You*

> *are to be holy to Me because I have set you apart from the nations to be My own* (20:22-24; 26).

Our God wants us to be different, to walk in the humility of obedience and in the beauty of holiness—the beauty of His Presence—because He wants us to be His own. He desires for us to be consecrated and devoted in love to Him alone, as a bride to her bridegroom. He longs to walk with us in growing intimacy and oneness of heart and mind.

---

[1] John 15:10

[2] Matthew 12:50

[3] John 15:12

Emor - אמר

Say

Leviticus 21:1–24:23; Ezekiel 44:15–31;
1 Peter 2:4–10

The original Hebrew name for *Vayikra*, the book of Leviticus, is *Torat Kohanim* (Instruction/Guidance for Priests). This portion is a perfect example of that designation. In the book of *Shemot*, Exodus, all the people of Israel are chosen and called to attain holiness–to be set apart from other nations by their unique, God-ordained lifestyle. In the *parasha*, as in the book of Vayikra generally, the exhortation is addressed particularly to the priests, *the sons of Aaron* (21:1), who are called to live at a higher level of devotion to God. They are set apart from the people to be the example of what a sanctified, dedicated life of holiness unto God looks like. They were to be role models; to illustrate the depth of intimacy it was possible to attain in covenant relationship with the God of Israel.

Shalom - Shabbat

Aaron, the High Priest, is known as *Rodef Shalom*—the Pursuer of Peace. The priests, or *kohanim*, as his descendants were to be those who constantly aspired to peace and reconciliation. God does not deny the reality of wars waged by broken humankind, and at times even the necessity of war in countering evil, but

He holds high His ideal of peace. Everything holy is a beacon for peace, for *Shalom*.

The Hebrew word *Shalom* conveys far more than the image we derive from the English word 'peace', as beautiful as that is. It is derived from the root word *shalem*, which means wholeness and completion. It is bound up with the word *shlemut*, perfection—the goal towards which we aspire, the hope that we are promised will be fulfilled in Messiah at the end of days. Perfection and wholeness will be restored in the day the *Sar Shalom*, the Prince of Peace, returns to reign and the knowledge of God covers the earth as the *waters cover the sea.*[1]

At the culmination of mankind's journey, when the Kingdom of God is established in all the earth, the realm that ensues is referred to in Jewish writings as "*the day that is all Shabbat.*" It will be an eternal timeless existence of peace and joy in the light and glory of His Presence. Until that marvelous day, God has set a special day in place whereupon, here and now, every week, we can enter in and enjoy the benefits of that future eternal day. The *Sabbath*—the sign of His covenant promise to us of the eternal Shabbat that He will establish at the end of time.

Shabbat is a gift of love from a faithful Father to His children; a day to spend especially with Him. It is a day set apart, when His Presence can be entered into and enjoyed in a deeper, intentional way. It is a day one is enabled, as it were, to pass beyond the veil of one's common weekly routine with its daily demands and to enter into the Holy of Holies. It is a time to delight in the beauty and intimacy of holiness. The gift is there every week at the appointed time; we need only receive and appropriate it.

Priests of God

They shall be holy to their God and not profane the Name of their God... (Leviticus 21:6). Those who serve God, the priests, are obligated to act in a way that honors and sanctifies His Name. This is called in Hebrew, *kiddush haShem* (sanctification of the Name). The obverse is called *chillul haShem* (desecration of the Name).

From the time of the Exodus, it was God's desire that His people be a "kingdom of priests". Each man was to be a priest and his home a small sanctuary—a holy dwelling for the Most High, where His blessing, peace and joy would abound. This could not be accomplished until they were spiritually and mentally set free, thus the need for the Tabernacle and the Temples. These became the house of God and a means of illustrating and teaching what the holy habitation of God's Presence was designed to be.

Yeshua came, the Temple was destroyed, and after His sacrificial, atoning death God raised Him up in the resurrection power of His Holy Spirit. He then became our great High Priest, our Mediator and Intercessor before the throne of God. In Him, we all are now called to be a holy priesthood whose lives are dedicated in service to the Almighty. In the authority of the Name of our High Priest, and empowered by the Holy Spirit, we are both priests—*kohanim*, who live to sanctify and glorify the Name of our Father God—and the living "temple" of His Presence on earth.

The Omer - 49 Days of Anticipation

The commandment to count seven full weeks from *Pesach*/ Passover to *Shavuot*/Pentecost is conveyed in Leviticus 23:15. On the second day of Passover a sheaf (*omer*) of grain, the first-fruits (*bikkurim*) of the barley harvest, is waved as an offering to the Lord and the counting of seven weeks begins. This period of "counting the Omer" links the celebration of God's redemption of His people to the commemoration of His revelation to us of His Presence and His Word at Sinai.

To establish a marriage covenant in ancient times, once the bride was chosen the prospective groom paid her father the required 'bride-price'. At Pesach the precious blood of the Lamb was shed and the great price was eternally paid for the

Bride of *Adonai* (the Lord). The first stage of betrothal is accomplished.

The betrothal ceremony was conducted forty-nine days later, when the prospective groom presented his bride with a written marriage contract, a *ketubah*. Likewise, Shavuot is the completion of the Exodus. The betrothal is sealed.

At the first Shavuot the marriage covenant of God and His Bride Israel was confirmed when He presented her with His Torah, the written promise of His love and fidelity and of His blessings of provision and protection. It was sealed with the guarantee of the Holy Spirit, who descended upon the people in tongues of fire. Again, at Shavuot/Pentecost on Mount Zion, the confirming fire of the Holy Spirit descended upon the disciples of Yeshua, who were eagerly awaiting that which was promised by their Risen Lord.

In place of the barley sheaf waved the day after Pesach, two fragrant loaves of bread were waved at Shavuot—the first-fruits of the wheat harvest, gathered from the crops that were watched with care during the seven weeks. The forty-nine day period of the Omer is a time of preparation and nurturing, when we carefully watch the 'fruit' growing in our own lives. We count the days in anticipation of a special meeting with our Beloved when we can offer Him the gift of the first-fruits of our labors.

Our "priestly" service, during this interim period of waiting for the return of our Beloved as He goes to "*prepare a place*"[2] for us in His Father's home, is an expression and outpouring of our love towards Him. Our deepest desire is to serve our Bridegroom-King with hope-filled anticipation and total devotion until He returns, at the final ingathering of the harvest. This will coincide with the ultimate appointed time of *Sukkot*/Tabernacles, *Zman Simchateinu*—the time of our Joy—when we will delight in the glorious celebration of the Wedding Feast.

---

1 Isaiah 11:9-10

2 John 14:2-3

Behar - בְּהַר

On Mount Sinai

Leviticus 25:1–26:2; Jeremiah 32:6–27;
I Peter 1:13–16

The Jubilee Year

At the heart of this week's portion is the visionary concept of returning land to its original owner at the end of a fifty year cycle. This prevents the polarization of society into two classes: wealthy and powerful landowners and permanently impoverished servants. In an agrarian society, such as Israel was in biblical times, a farmer who sold his land in order to pay debts had no prospect of ever being more than a servant. His children, too, would be trapped at the level of servitude.

In the light of this human misfortune and social instability, God's plan of the Jubilee year—called *Yovel* in Hebrew—offered hope and opportunity to all. In the fiftieth year any land that had been sold would be returned to its original owners. The buyer had, in effect, been leasing the land. Two spiritual principles are made evident by this plan:

1. All the earth, in a general sense, but specifically the Land of Israel and its inhabitants, belong to God. Individuals do not have the right to permanently possess either the land or people.

2. No human being should be condemned to permanent servitude or slavery. A way should always be available whereby he can be reinstated to a position of dignity.

Some critics have scorned the concept of a Jubilee year as being impossible to implement; however, archaeologists have found records of deeds from the late biblical period containing references to it being in operation.

The first Ashkenazi Chief Rabbi of Palestine (as Israel was called at the time of his tenure) Rav Avraham Yitzchak Kook taught that the basis for the Jubilee, *Yovel*, was spiritual rather than economical. God intended that it should restore a sense of unity to Israel, in the understanding that all are equal in His sight. Thus people would be encouraged to value and respect one another. Also, it would restore self-respect to the person who had sunk into poverty.

Just as the weekly Shabbat offers the opportunity to re-orientate oneself and see oneself in non-economic terms, so the *Shmi'tah* every seven years and the Jubilee year every fifty (after 7x7) would enable the entire society to put aside economic competition in order to realize the true inner value of every individual.

The Shmi'tah Year

The *Shmi'tah* year is described in Leviticus 25:2, where it is recorded that in every seventh year no work is to be done on the land, "the land rests". The Hebrew word *ve'shavtah* is derived from the root *shin*, *bet*, *tav*—also the root of *Shabbat*. The phrase can also be read as: the land "returns" to the Lord.

There is a similarity between the Hebrew verbs to rest and to return that is worth considering. As His people we rest in Him in a special way on the seventh day. The stillness, the inner settling, returns us to our source—to the One who created us and in whom we find blessing. The Land is to rest during the seventh year. The land is thus personified. It too grows tired and depleted and requires rest and refreshing.[1] The Holy Land, like the holy people who inhabit it, needs a Shabbat to replenish itself and to bear witness to God's ownership of it. God promises to provide for and to sustain directly during the Sabbatical years, just as He does for Shabbat.

It is of interest to note that these agricultural laws of Shmi'tah and Jubilee were given at Sinai, in the wilderness, where no one owned land. All were of equal status at the foot of the Mount. Thus the implementation of these laws, in addition to the other physical and spiritual benefits, is also a powerful reminder of the equality of the people of God and of the "*unity that commands a blessing*"[2]. This unity is forged as a result of walking together in His ways, in loving obedience and in recognition of His authority. Only then will His dew of refreshing settle like anointing oil upon our lives, in our families, as a community, and even as a nation.

The Call of the Shofar

The journey from redemption at Passover to revelation at Shavuot/Pentecost was seven weeks, the forty-nine days of the Omer. The fiftieth day, a day of *yovel*, or jubilee, was the day the mountain trembled at the sound of the *shofar* (ram's horn or trumpet) of the Lord and fire flashed forth and a cloud of glory covered the Mount. God spoke and revealed Himself to His people and presented them with His Word, the Torah.

A note of interest regarding the shofar: The horn with which a shepherd summoned his flock home was called a *yovel*, probably based on the root meaning of the word, which is "to bring". A literal meaning of the word *yovel* is "bringing people or things home", or restoring them to their proper place in God's order of things. We see in Joshua 6:4-8, for example, along with a remarkable pattern of sevens, that the horns blown by the priests are called *shofarot hayovelim*. The collapse of the walls was a response to the summons of the yovel, and Jericho was the first city to "come home" to its rightful, God-ordained owners.[3]

After Yeshua's ascension the disciples gathered, as was their custom, to celebrate Shavuot at the Temple in Jerusalem. They were celebrating the giving of the Word of God, the Torah, and also the Word made flesh, the Living Torah. The God of Israel revealed Himself once again and, as before, tongues of fire were visible as His Holy Spirit came to rest on His people. Shavuot connects Mount Sinai (Exodus 19) and Mount Zion (Acts 2). The Word Incarnate, according to the New Covenant promised in Jeremiah 31:33, has given us the gift of the Holy Spirit who has written the Torah on our hearts and who enables us to walk in the ways of God according to His will. For His eternal glory!

---

1 See Exodus 23:10-11.

2 Psalm 133:1

3 It is of historical interest to note that Jericho was the first city claimed and fully taken over by Yasser Arafat, as leader of the "Palestinian Liberation" Organization. The claim has been extended in succession to other major biblically Jewish cities along the backbone of Israel, e.g. Hebron, the city of the patriarchs, (where Abraham and Sarah, Isaac and Rebekah, Jacob and Leah are buried), Shechem (Nablus), where Joseph is buried, Bethlehem, where King David, Boaz, and Yeshua were born, and where Rachel and Ruth are buried. Their goal, God forbid, is the 'crown' of Jerusalem—the place the God of Israel has chosen as His dwelling place, forever.

Bechukotai - בחקתי

In My Statutes

Leviticus 26:3–27:34; Jeremiah 16:19–17:14;
Luke 4:16–21

The opening verse of *Bechukotai* is directly translated from the Hebrew Scriptures as:

> *If you will walk in My statutes (bechukotai) and keep My commandments (mitzvot) and carry them out…[then] I will grant your rains in their season, so that the earth shall yield its pro duce and the trees of the field their fruit* (26:3-4).

A remarkable connection is made between the laws of nature and the Law, or Torah, of God. There is an indication that the productivity of the earth depends upon whether God's Word is being studied and walked out in obedience in the lives of His people. The knowledge that all of Creation was breathed into existence by God—He spoke "and it was so"—lends understanding to the concept that it is also by His Word that the same Creation is maintained.

We read in Paul's beautiful eulogy of Yeshua in the first chapter of Colossians:

> *He is supreme over all creation, because in connection with Him were created all things—in heaven and on earth, visible and invisible, whether thrones, lordships, rulers [of nations] or authorities—they have all been created through Him and for Him. He existed before all things, and He holds everything together*[1].

The same Yeshua, the Word made flesh who dwelt among us, is the One who was there at the creation of all and now holds all things together.

It is the Word, the Torah, of the Father that Yeshua embodies and came to fulfill—to fill full of meaning. Those who follow Him or literally 'walk' after Him are enabled by the Spirit of God to walk in paths of righteousness and peace. We see the promise of this in Ezekiel 36:27, where we notice an important repetition of the opening words of this parasha:

> *I will put My Spirit within you and cause [enable] you to walk* ***in My statutes****, and you will be careful to observe My ordinances.*

Blessed or Cursed?

The parasha contains a section on blessings and curses, which is echoed in the haftarah: *Blessed is the man who trusts in the Lord, and whose hope is in the Lord*[2]. On the other hand, *Cursed is the man who trusts in man and makes flesh His strength, whose heart departs from the Lord* (17:5).

The Lord sees where the trust of one's heart rests. As we choose to place our hope fully and firmly in Him, let us always remember: *God's blessing makes life rich; nothing we do can improve on God.*[3]

Rabbi S.R. Hirsch proposes in his inspiring commentary, *The Pentateuch,* that the departure of one's heart from the Lord in increasing coldness, and the corresponding defection from His ways, is not a sudden thing but an increasingly downward spiral. He records five stages of defection:

1. Neglect of the Word. The failure to study the Word of God leads to carelessness in hearing and obeying God's will.
2. Forsaking the practice of God's ways.
3. Contempt of the Word and for those who obey it. Ignorance leads to contempt.

4. Hatred and direct opposition of those faithful to God and active denial of the validity of the Word.
5. Denial of the existence of God. In doing so, the person *"breaks My covenant"* (26:15).

As a result of neglect and then denial of the fundamental truth of God's Word, one ultimately denies God's existence and "breaks the last slender thread that still binds the defector to the covenant of God."[4] In so doing he brings the increasing weight of curses upon himself. As we have too painfully seen and experienced in history, for Israel as a people the final curse results in exile from the land and persecution among the nations. Consequently, the land itself suffers desolation (27:32-33).

Restoration

God, in His great mercy, leaves a way of repentance and restoration for His people: *...If their uncircumcised hearts are humbled, and they accept their guilt, then I will remember My covenant...and...I will remember the land* (26:41-42). The Sages say, in agreement with the Word, that the Land, the people, and the Scriptures of Israel are inextricably intertwined. This can explain why all three are under constant and hostile attack by the enemies of the God of Israel.

Jeremiah foretells that, in the unfolding of God's great redemptive purposes, the Gentiles from the ends of the earth would come to the LORD, and He would cause them to know Him (16:19-21). The prophet Zechariah also describes:

> *...the nations shall go up ...to keep the Feast of Tabernacles. Whichever of the families of the earth do not come up to Jerusalem to worship the King, the LORD of hosts, on them there will be no rain.*[5]

Thus we see that the destinies of the nations, and their fruitfulness, are also connected to and bound up with the Land, and the Scriptures, and the people of Israel.

Chazak, chazak, ve'nitchazek!
Be strong, be strong, and let us strengthen one another!

---

[1] Colossians 1:15–17, *Complete Jewish Bible*, David Stern.

[2] Jeremiah17:7

[3] Proverbs 10:22, *The Message*, Eugene Peterson.

[4] Rabbi S.R. Hirsch, *The Pentateuch*, commentary on *Bechukotai.*

[5] Zechariah 14:17

NUMBERS

B'MIDBAR - בְּמִדבר

The Wilderness - Place of Revelation

It is somehow strange that the barren, waterless wilderness is chosen by God as the setting for spiritual revelation. And yet, as we see described in the book of Exodus, the shepherd Moses is drawn there like a magnet.

> *And Moses... led the flock far away into the desert, and came to the mountain of God, to Horeb* (Exodus 3:10).

There he encounters the living God, who speaks to him from a bush that is burning and yet not consumed.

In response to this call of God, Moses becomes a leader of his people Israel. He is God's agent for defeating the tyranny of Pharaoh and redeeming the Israelites from slavery in Egypt. Once again Moses leads his "flock" into the wilderness and returns to the same mountain, Horeb in Sinai. There, now as a people, the former slaves experience a dramatic revelation of the God of their fathers Abraham, Isaac and Jacob. And they receive the gift of His Torah. The hope is given, by His glorious Presence and the revelation of His Word, for redemption from the enslaving bonds of sin and the restoration of mankind's lost purity. The means is provided whereby they can once again begin to walk in the delight and fullness of covenant relationship with their Father God.

To impress upon them the importance of this encounter and covenant, God instructs His people to remember these mighty acts of His redemption and revelation on a regular basis. He sets appointed times of rememberance, celebration and communal meeting with Him in an annual Festival Cycle. The biblical narrative of their journey through the wilderness relates, however, that Israel often chafes at the "yoke" of His Kingship. They choose to rebel against His instructions and they forget their God.

This has been the tendency of the children of God throughout history as we struggle to overcome our inherent rebellious nature. Yet even when Israel forgets Him, God never forgets, and He faithfully reminds His people of His Presence and His love through His Word and His prophets.

In the book of *Vayikra* (Leviticus) a vision of the ideal "kingdom of priests" walking in holiness before God was delineated. Now in *B'midbar* (Numbers) we find the down-to-earth reality of people as they really are: weak, complaining and often annoying! We discover that the transition from slavery to royalty is not instantaneous. It requires the journey through the wilderness. It happens *B'midbar*.

B'midbar - במדבר
In the Wilderness

Numbers 1:1–4:20; Hosea 2:1–22;
1 Corinthians 21:12–20

When God created man He placed him in a garden—*Gan Eden.* The Garden of Eden was a beautiful setting for this beloved creation of God. It was a place traversed by flowing, sparkling waters and filled with lush foliage and flora of dazzling color—pleasing to all the senses. The rigors of demanding work and any struggle against the elements were unknown. Man and beast lived in tranquil unity and the Spirit of God permeated the entire expanse. It was ideal. It was paradise.

The desert wilderness encountered in the book of *B'midbar* appears as the very antithesis of Gan Eden. All its elements seem in opposition to man. It is either too hot or too cold. It is desolate; seemingly empty and barren of life. A place devoid of hope. The desert in which the Israelites find themselves is described in Deuteronomy 8:15 as:

> *... a great and terrible wilderness, with venomous serpents and scorpions, and waterless, thirsty ground.*

The Place of Revelation

Perhaps this extreme environment renders it the perfect place for man to meet again with his Creator God. The barrenness reflects the effect of sin on the soul—a spiritual dryness and withering of fruitfulness and life. This realization should serve to draw one back to God's ways of wholeness and spiritual abundance. As basic supplies are scarce, and self-preservation is of paramount concern, the wilderness is a place where God can make evident His Divine protection and daily provision of sustenance.

The objective of the wilderness journey is to afford man the opportunity to develop trust in God on a daily basis. The stark illustration of the desert landscape mirrors the futility of man's strivings and self-dependence; nonetheless God meets him there and He provides man with the vision and the means to reverse the curse he brought upon himself in the Garden. Hope was restored at Sinai in the revelation of His glorious Presence and the gift of His eternal Word.

Almost incredibly, we later learn that after their dramatic, miraculous exodus from Egypt and their witnessing of the power and provision of God first-hand, the people of Israel rise up in contention and complain against Him. How little human nature seems to have changed. In spite of receiving our Father's wondrous gift of His Word, and its affirmation and incarnation in Yeshua, we often rebel today—just as the Israelites did then. We go our own way and forget Him. Nevertheless, the Lord faithfully reminds us: *"I remember you… your love like a bride, when you followed Me in the wilderness, in a land not sown"*.[1] He constantly woos us with His love and gives us the opportunity again and again to draw close to His side, where we belong.

This book of Numbers describes a people facing the challenges of a spiritual as well as a geographical wilderness. After their great deliverance from the bondage of slavery, they find themselves in the daily routine and discipline of desert life. Concurrently, the focus of leadership shifts from Moses to Aaron, the High Priest. The prophet speaks forth mighty proclamations and revelations from the mountain top, "...whereas the priest is involved with the people in the complexities and routines of daily life."[2]

These events give us pause to consider that the deeper lessons of life, the objective of which is the building of covenant relationship with God and with others, are learned not in the grand, auspicious events of our lives but in the undistinguished times of ordinary moments.

"How goodly are your tents O Jacob!"

The Sanctuary of the Ark of the Covenant was the center around which the camp of the Israelites was deployed. Every individual tent was situated in relation to the Tabernacle. The Tent of the Lord, housing His Word and His Presence at its heart, was therefore the first thing one saw when leaving one's tent and the point of reference one used to return home. The Tabernacle represented one's communal identity as the people of God.

Closer to home one would identify with the banner of one's tribe. The symbol on each banner was related to the prophetic words of Jacob on his deathbed, where he prophesied regarding the destinies of his sons, each the head of one of the twelve tribes. The banners were signs of one's calling and redemptive purposes in the plan of God for mankind.

In spite of their general tendency to murmur and complain, it is worthy of note that the people of Israel conducted themselves in an orderly fashion in the ongoing process of encamping and packing up and moving. At least in this process there was no jealousy evidenced, no struggle for position, and no argument about who went first or who camped where. They accepted God's direction through their leaders and this enormous task was accomplished smoothly, in harmony and peaceful order.

Israel - Beloved Bride

The *haftarah* this week, Hosea 2:1-23, encapsulates the essence of *B'midbar.* The prophet presents a striking and evocative picture of the Sinai Covenant as a marriage bond between God and Israel. The nation, like an unfaithful wife, has turned away from her husband and in a state of apostasy has shamelessly gone lusting after false gods. They have thus caused themselves to be called "*Not My people*" (*Lo Ammi*) (1:9; 2:1) and "*Denied compassion*" (*Lo Ruchama*) (1:6). However, in His unswerving compassion and eternal love, the Lord her faithful husband extends hope for restoration and an assurance that His Divine mercy transcends judgment for her sin.

Finally, in a God-initiated renewal of the covenant, He says that they again will be "*My people*" *(Ammi)* and "*Accorded compassion*" (*Ruchama*) (2:23). He will coax His beloved into the wilderness—a realm symbolizing spiritual rebirth for all who are cognizant of the need for covenantal renewal. There He will speak to her tenderly and once more lead her to Himself, to a place of hope and fruitfulness and safety.

Verses 19 and 20 present powerful words of espousal that convey the everlasting, unwavering commitment of God's love for His people. These words are recited to this day in prayer by observant Jews as they daily and faithfully bind the leather straps of the *tefillin* (phylacteries) around the arm and fingers of one hand; a symbolic reminder of a wedding band. In response to the loving initiative of God, they "bind" themselves to Him in an act of faith and hope.

> *And I will betroth you to me forever. I will espouse you in righteousness and justice, in love and compassion. I will betroth you in faithfulness, and you will acknowledge [know and be devoted to] the* LORD.

We can stand confidently on the wonderful promise of God in Hosea 3:5,

> *Afterward the Israelites will return and seek their God and David their king* [the King of kings, *Mashiach ben David,* Messiah son of David]. *They will come trembling to the* Lord, *and to His blessings in the last days.*

---

[1] Jeremiah 2:2

[2] *Etz Hayim* Torah and Commentary, JPS, 769.

Nasso - נשא

Take a Census

Numbers 4:21–7:89; Judges 13:2–25;
John 12:20–36

The Hebrew verb form *nasso* is frequently used in the first two portions of the book *B'midbar* (Numbers). It is usually translated "count" but the literal meaning is "uplift"—to ennoble, to elevate. *Nissuin,* from the same root word, is the Hebrew term for marriage. During a Jewish marriage celebration it is customary for the bride and groom to be lifted up on chairs accompanied by joyous cheering. This symbolizes the spiritual uplifting of two individuals who are now united, body and spirit, in the noble purposes of God. In the portions of *B'midbar* and *Nasso* the census counts the individuals who are to serve in the uplifting and sacred task of guarding and caring for the Sanctuary of God and its holy contents.

This portion usually falls during the Omer—a time of counting the forty-nine days between Passover and Shavuot. As 'priests' who serve in His Kingdom, it is a time for taking spiritual stock and preparing oneself for what God desires to reveal regarding one's spiritual growth and the direction of one's life. Just as He did when He revealed Himself to His people at Sinai, God meets with us with specific intent in order to lift us up! He strengthens and enables us to stand upright in Him by the power of His Spirit.

Confession and Forgiveness

> *When a man or woman commits any wrong toward a fellow man, thus breaking faith with the Lord, and that person realizes his guilt, he shall confess the wrong that he has done. He shall make restitution...* (Numbers 5:5-7a).

We see clearly in these verses that any offense toward another, who bears the image of God, is a breach of faith against the Creator Himself. To cheat or act wrongly toward another, whether by thought, word or deed, is not only a crime but also is a profanation of the Name of God. The victim's faith in the goodness of God is undermined, and his trust in the decency of his fellow man is shaken.

By God's grace, if the person who has committed an offense realizes his guilt there is a means of righting the wrong. Firstly by confession—the wrong needs to be articulated to the victim. The reflexive Hebrew verb used here, *hitvadu*, indicates that the focus of the confession is first to oneself before God; who bears witness that it comes from a sincere heart and is not merely an outward expression. On this basis we confess our sin to those whom we have wronged and from whom we ask forgiveness. We then actively make any possible restitution, for example restoring any misappropriated property plus 20% of its value (5:7b).

Sotah - The Suspected Adulteress

The text moves immediately to the description of an interesting and potentially terrifying and demeaning ritual to which a jealous husband could submit his wife if he suspected her of adultery. In an elaborate ceremony, the priest would prepare the "*waters of bitterness*" (5:18), which the *sotah* would drink. If she was guilty of unfaithfulness the effects of the water would be painful and obvious to the community and she would be ostracized. The juxtaposition with the former verses causes an awareness of the severity of the crime of betrayal in marriage. Other transgressions, apart from murder, can be made right but after adultery it is almost impossible, without God's grace, to restore the marriage to its former state of trust.

Marriage is considered the holiest state in the eyes of God and it is also the foundation of social order. It was therefore beneficial to have a means to clarify the suspicion in the husband's mind as well as to afford protection to the wife in the event of unreasonable jealousy on the part of the husband. Rabbi S.R Hirsch points out: "Only if the husband has never been guilty of unchastity can he impose this ordeal on his wife."[1] He accentuates the fact that God's laws of morality apply equally to both men and women.

The Talmud records that this ritual was only effective at the time that people believed in its ability to reveal guilt and innocence (Sotah 9:9). After the destruction of the Second Temple, and at a time when it seems consciences were more seared and people more cynical, it was discarded. This supernatural "trial" was thus still in effect at the time of Yeshua. How much more poignant and meaningful the account of His meeting with the adulteress at the well becomes[2] when one realizes that instead of bitter waters He offers her the Living Waters of the good news of God that bring eternal life and blessing.[3]

Birkat Kohanim - The Priestly Blessing

The well-known and beautiful priestly blessing is found in this week's parasha (6:24-26). Today, it is recited by *Kohanim* in synagogues on Shabbat and often by parents to their children on *Erev Shabbat* (Friday night).

It is a three-part petition, in response to which one trusts the Lord's blessing:

1. **May the Lord bless you and keep you.**
   This petition is for physical blessing and protection. The blessing includes financial prosperity; with the understanding that one will be kept from the corruption of wealth.

2. **May the Lord cause the light of His face to shine upon you, and be gracious to you.**

   The light of the Lord is associated with His Word and truth.[4] The petition carries the blessing that one be filled with the ever-increasing "light" of knowledge of His Word and truth. Knowledge alone "puffs up." Implicit in the petition is a plea for His gracious gift of understanding and for the wisdom to apply the Word in one's life in humility and grace towards others.

   The blessing also conveys the Lord's pleasure in seeing each of His children, as Rabbi Hertz comments: "To cause the face to shine upon one is the biblical idiom for being friendly towards him."[5] One's face lights up when one sees a friend!

3. **May the Lord lift up His countenance to you, and give you peace.**

   The final petition is for a constant awareness of the Lord's presence—that He not hide His face from one. It culminates in the wonderful blessing in which all of one's life should be rooted, His peace—His *Shalom*.

Another Hebrew word from the same root as *shalom* is *shleimut*—wholeness and completeness, which is the fullness of peace. True fullness of peace is to be found in the *Sar Shalom*, the Prince of Peace, Yeshua, who assures us:

> *Peace I leave with you; My peace I give to you. Not as the world gives do I give to you. Let not your hearts be troubled, neither let them be afraid.*[6]

Paul, the apostle to the nations, offers this blessing that indeed carries an echo of the Aaronic priestly blessing:

> *Grace to you and peace from God our Father and the Lord Jesus Christ.*
>
> *Blessed be the God and Father of our Lord Yeshua the Messiah, who has blessed us in Messiah with every spiritual blessing in the heavenly places, even as he chose us in him before the foundation of the world, that we should be holy and blameless before him.*
>
> *In love he predestined us for adoption through Messiah Yeshua, according to the purpose of his will, to the praise of his glorious grace, with which he has blessed us in the Beloved.*[7]

---

[1] Hirsch, Rabbi Samson Raphael, *The Pentateuch*, Feldheim Publishers, Jerusalem, NY, *Nasso*.

[2] John 4:9-42

[3] This connection is highlighted in FFOZ's (First Fruits of Zion), Torah Club, Volume 4.

[4] E.g., Proverbs 6:23.

[5] Hertz, Rabbi Dr. J.H., *The Pentateuch and Haftorahs*, Second Edition, Soncino Press, 595.

[6] John 14:27

[7] Ephesians 1:2-6

Beha'alotkha - בהעלותך

When you set up [the lamps]

Numbers 8:1 – 12:16; Zechariah 2:10 – 4:7;
1 Corinthians 10:1-13

The *parasha* this week opens with a description of the *menorah*—the seven-branched lampstand. The menorah has been a central symbol in Judaism as it represents the *Etz Chaim*, the Tree of Life—the Torah, the Word of God. In modern times it is the symbol for the re-birthed State of Israel.

The Tree of Light - The Menorah

The menorah was the predominant piece of furniture in the Holy Place of the Tabernacle. It was situated before the southern wall, to the left of Aaron the High Priest when he entered. His priestly duty was to light the seven lamps of the menorah every morning and evening. This light was to be a *ner tamid*, literally a 'constant candle' or eternal light. The light symbolized the radiance of the Presence of God, the illumination and beauty of His Word of truth, and His constant care and watchfulness over His people. The Vilna Gaon (1720–1797), a great spiritual and intellectual leader in Eastern Europe, is recorded as saying:

> When Aaron lit the menorah his attitude never changed. Day after day, year after year, he approached this duty with the

> same sense of reverence and awe that he brought to it on the first day.

Aaron, no doubt, had a deep appreciation of all the menorah symbolized and retained a vision for the prophetic activity of setting up (preparing) and lighting the lamps.

The Talmud records an interesting *midrash*:

> Israel said before God, "Lord of the Universe Thou commandest us to illumine before Thee; art Thou not the Light of the world, and with Whom light dwelleth?"
>
> "Not that I require your light," was the Divine reply, "but that you may perpetuate the light which I conferred on you as an example to the nations of the world"[1]

This, of course, refers to the call of Israel to be a light to the nations. They are to be a witness to the One true God and spread the good news of His Kingship and the light of His Word, depicted in the menorah.

> *You are my servant, Israel, in whom I will display My splendor… I will also make you a light for the Gentiles, that you may bring my salvation to the ends of the earth* (Isaiah 49:3 & 6b).

The splendor of God's glory was first revealed to Israel at Sinai and dwelt among them in the Holy of Holies, where it rested above the Ark of the Covenant that housed the tablets of His Word. It was the menorah, however, that stood as the reminder that His truth was to be shared and lifted up as a beacon to draw all nations from darkness into its glorious light.

The menorah has branches and is decorated with almond blossoms and leaf shaped lamps. The description "tree of light" is therefore fitting. It is reminiscent of the Tree of Life in the Garden of Eden and, as a symbol of the Word of God, it anticipates the full Redemption of the world. It heralds the time when there will no longer be any curse and the Tree of Life will stand resplendent with fruit in the City of the Great King, Jerusalem.

> *And the leaves of the tree are for the healing of the nations. The throne of God and of the Lamb will be in the city, and His servants will serve Him.*[2]

Yeshua, as the Living Torah, the "Word Who became flesh and dwelt among us," was indeed lifted up on a tree as a banner for the nations. In Him, the Lamb of God, all may find healing and be delivered from the darkness of the curse of sin and death and come into the light and life of the eternal Kingdom of God.

The Blessing of Unity

Two interesting facts among countless concerning the menorah are: (a) It is the only piece of the Tabernacle furnishings that God commands to be made of one solid block of beaten gold[3]; and (b) Aaron is commanded by God to arrange the wicks of the lamps toward the front of the central shaft so that they will emit one combined blaze of light (8:1-2). The picture here is one of unity. We need to shine wherever the Lord places us, "…like a little candle…you in your small corner and I in mine," but our light shines more brightly when it is connected with other lights.

As priests of the Almighty God we are encouraged to nurture daily and keep the light of truth lit within us—the new life in Yeshua—with the oil of the Holy Spirit. Just as the lamps of the menorah, as we each focus on the "Light of the World" Himself and are united under His leadership, our combined light will indeed shine more brightly for the Father's glory.

Yeshua, who said: *"I am the light of the world; he who follows Me will not walk in darkness, but will have the light of life"*[4], also exhorts us: "*Let your* [plural] *light shine before men in such a way that they may see your* [plural] *good works and glorify your Father Who is in heaven*"[5].

Seven Flames

The *haftarah* (prophetic reading) this week beautifully and powerfully emphasizes the main themes of the *parasha*. The prophet returns with the exiles from Babylon, after king Cyrus issued his decree permitting the Jews to return to Jerusalem. They do so under the leadership of Zerubavel and Joshua the High Priest, with the aim to restore the ruined Temple of God.

Zechariah's God-given vision and message are intended to encourage the people who are overcome with fear of the enemies who oppose them and are balking at the physical obstacles in their way. They are exhorted to see the larger picture of their calling, and to rise above their human weaknesses and be strengthened in the knowledge that they will succeed: "*Not by might, nor by power, but by My Spirit,*" *says the Lord* (4:6).

In Hebrew this verse is written: *Loh b'chayil ve'loh ve'kho'ach ki im b'ruchi.* Seven words, which correspond with the seven flames of the menorah—the Tree of Life, the Living Word, filled with the pure oil of the Spirit of holiness. In this powerful light of the truth of God, nothing is impossible.

---

1 Dr. J.H.Hertz, *Pentateuch and Haftorahs*, The Soncino Press, 605.

2 Revelation 22:2-3

3 Exodus 25:36

4 John 8:12

5 Matthew 5:16

Shlach Lekha - שלח לך

Send Thou

Numbers 13:1 – 15:41; Joshua 2:1-24;
Hebrews 3:7-19

"Send thou – *Shlach lekha,*" the directive God gives Moses carries an echo of the command, "Go thou—*Lekh lekha,*" which God gave directly to Abraham when He sent him forth from his native land to "*a land that I will show you*"[1]. The same Land that He swore to give to him and his promised descendants forever[2]. The difference at the outset of the two scenarios is that Abraham did not know the location of his destination and he set out in pure trust and faith in the One Who sent him. Moses and the Israelites, the descendants of Abraham, Isaac and Jacob, knew exactly where it was.

We know that Abraham journeyed and arrived and dwelt in the Land of promise. The narrative of *B'midbar* (Numbers) presents us with the sad reality that the adult generation of those who left Egypt, with the exception of Joshua and Caleb, do not. They become known as *dor hamidbar* – the wilderness generation. They never leave the wilderness and it becomes the place of their death and burial.

The frustrations and challenges of the wilderness are intended to refine and prepare them for the responsibility of being an *am segullah* (a precious, treasured people) chosen by God for His purposes. Sadly, they succumb to resentment and negativity. As a result, fear replaces faith and doubt replaces trust in God's Word and leading. Rather than looking forward in faith and in anticipation of the new thing God is doing, they long for the old ways of Egypt. They look back to the place of their slavery and are blinded to the potential of the present.

The Sin of the Ten Spies

The incident of the Spies is a major turning point in the lives of the wilderness generation. The description at the start of the *parasha* tells us that the group was comprised of choice candidates: "*...a man from every tribe... every one a prince among them*" (13:2). The twelve names are then listed, underscoring their importance. Among them we notice Caleb, representative of the tribe of Judah, and Hoshea of the tribe of Ephraim. Significantly, we are told that Moses changes the name of the one who had been his assistant from the start and who would eventually replace him as leader. A letter from the Divine Name is added and *Hoshea* (save) becomes *Yehoshua* (The LORD saves), a form of the word *Yeshuah*, which means Salvation. Yehoshua (Joshua) and Caleb prove to be the only two of the group who retain their faith and trust in the Word of God and they ultimately lead the new generation of Israelites into the Promised Land.

Moses dispatches the twelve men into Canaan to explore it from a strategic point of view. Their task is to gain information on the cities and fortifications and to learn of the nature of the inhabitants. They are also instructed to bring back samples of the "*fruit of the land*" (13:20). After forty days they return from their mission and instead of presenting objective facts the majority of ten gives a subjective opinion and they bemoan the impossibility of victory. This bad report utterly demoralizes the people. They are struck with fear and their faith in the power of God is undermined.

Caleb attempts to calm the people and proclaims: "*We should go up at once and possess it; for we are well able to overcome it*" (13:30). He knew God was with them and He was able. No further preparation on their part would make any difference. But the people are deaf to this truth and hear the word of the ten spies who have looked to man and their own strength. They report: "*...we were in our own sight as grasshoppers, and so were we in their sight*" (13:33). Although they are the redeemed, chosen "princes" of God, they see themselves as insects!

The sin of the spies includes cowardice, complaining, self-pity and rebellion; but, more than that, it is a rebellion against God Himself and the rejection of the faith and trust in Him affirmed by Moses, Aaron, Joshua and Caleb.

The Song of the Grapes

One of the many impressive biblical images is that of two men carrying a giant cluster of grapes on a pole between them. It is the logo of the Ministry of Tourism in the modern State of Israel, signifying the bounty and beauty of this "good and promised land". We are told in the Hebrew text that the time of year the spies went into Canaan was *bikurei anavim*, the time of the *first-fruits of the grapes* (13:20). This would be mid-summer, during July and August. In response to Moshe's request to bring back fruits of the land they brought a selection of pomegranates and figs, and *a branch with one cluster of grapes.*

The branch from which the cluster grew is called *z'morah* in Hebrew, the root of which is *zemer*—a song. The hint here is that the "fruit of the Land" is more than mere produce. It also carries the "song" of the Land—its heart and essence, as it were. It is evidence of God's blessing upon and Presence in the place He has chosen and promised as an inheritance to His people.

Perhaps Joshua and Caleb were the two who volunteered to carry the grapes; no doubt a heavy burden in the heat of summer. Yet in their care of and proximity to the fruit they heard the song of the Land and their eyes of faith remained focused upon the *anavim* (grapes) and not upon the *anakim* (giants) of the enemy! One needs spiritual eyes and ears of faith in the God of Israel to hear the Song of the Land. The same challenge faces us today.

---

1 Genesis 12:1

2 Genesis 17:8

Korach - קרח

Korach

Numbers 16:1–18:32; 1 Samuel 11:14–12:22;
2 Timothy 2:14–25

Korach is the figure in the spotlight this week and the *parasha* carries his name. There are two groups involved in the rebellion against Moses and Aaron. The group more focused on "dethroning" Moses is led by Dathan and Abiram, of the tribe of Reuben. Theirs was the tribe of the first-born of Jacob and they believed that according to birthright, the rulers of Israel should be chosen from their ranks.

The group led by Korach is of the tribe of Levi. We see in the opening verse that Korach is the son of Izhar, who was the son of Kohath. Moses and Aaron's father, Amram, was also a son of Kohath. Thus they and Korach were cousins. It appears that jealousy and resentment over his cousins' appointments to positions of status are at the root of Korach's dispute. In particular, he believes that as a leader of the Levites he has as much right as Aaron to be honored as High Priest.

As the narrative unfolds we see clearly that this dispute is not conducive to peace and is displeasing to God. Arguments over issues, and occasions of controversy are unavoidable in any community. There are, however, elements whereby even a disagreement can render honor to our Father in heaven. Unfortunately this was not the case in Korach's contention; with dire consequences.

"Controversy for the Sake of Heaven"

Pirkei Avot (The Sayings, or Ethics, of the Fathers) is a compact and outstanding collection of Jewish wisdom. Avot 5:16 states:

> An example of a controversy for the sake of heaven is a disagreement between Hillel and Shammai, while one that is not for the sake of heaven is the argument of Korach and his followers.

Hillel and Shammai were renowned rabbis of the Second Temple period. Each founded a school devoted to Torah learning and the expounding of *halakha* (the detailed oral laws and observances that govern daily life). Traditionally *Beit Shammai* (literally the House [of learning] of Shammai) held to stricter, more conservative rulings, whereas *Beit Hillel* was more lenient and flexible in its decisions. In general the rulings of Hillel were more widely accepted. Yeshua was a contemporary of the revered grandson of Hillel, Rabbi Gamaliel (under whom the apostle Paul studied), and Yeshua's teachings reflected many of Beit Hillel's views. Although Hillel and Shammai disagreed on many complicated spiritual issues, it is recorded that they continued to consider one another as friends and at times enjoyed Shabbat dinners together. The Talmud also comments, "Beit Shammai did not refrain from marrying women from Beit Hillel"[1]. Their dispute was based on respect and friendship and thus honored God.

The heart of this positive disagreement is that the parties involved each upheld the ethic, "*Love truth and peace*"[2]. The distinctive elements of a controversy for the sake of Heaven may be described as follows:

1. The aim of the process is the search for truth and justice in accord with the will and Word of God.

2. The dialogue does not preclude or endanger the possibility of "loving one another" at its conclusion or thereafter.
3. The result should be the establishing of deeper relationship with God and one another in friendship and *shalom*—peace.

Controversy of Opposing Forces

In the world we see widespread, seemingly unending, painful conflict that is clearly not "for the sake of Heaven". The Sages of Israel traced the root of disagreement back to the second day of Creation, when God separated the waters into two different places. They held that even when similar substance is divided into two separate entities, the immediate result is the possibility of opposition and controversy. In other words, the creation of the power to love and the opportunity for creative relationship carried with it the opposing alternative of disagreement, hatred and destructive rebellion.

This adds an interesting dimension to the fact that woman was separated from man; Israel was separated from the nations; the Levites were separated from Israel; Moses and Aaron were separated from the Levites—and Korach & Co. rose up in rebellion! The harmony of unity, of 'one-ness', is shattered when we're faced with conflict that springs from human brokenness. The sins of pride, jealousy, unfounded hate, greed and seeking after position, power and prestige hold sway. The basis, and result, is not "truth and peace".

Another word from the root of *shalom* is *shleimut*, completeness or wholeness. When two groups, or two individuals (as in a marriage), can see each other not as an opposing obstacle or threat but rather as a complementary "other", with whom positive co-operation would lead to the development and completeness of both, then there is hope for interaction that honors their Creator. They can then participate in making the world a better place with the authority of the King of the Universe and in His love.

Sar Shalom - The Prince of Peace

It is worth considering that this great dividing wall of sin—of innate hostility against the "other"—is at the root of every sad and broken relationship, as well as every war and murderous feud of history. It is this 'dividing wall' that Yeshua Himself came to suffer and die and offer His life to atone for. And, in God's resurrection power, He gained the victory and became the Gate that offers the way through the 'wall', whereby all may find reconciliation and peace.

Our hope, as new creations aspiring to live lives of *shalom*, completeness and love one to another, lies in the Prince of Peace. *"For He Himself is our peace, Who has made the two one and has destroyed the barrier, the dividing wall of hostility."* [3]

In Yeshua, we can go throught the Gate and walk in His ways by the power of His Spirit. We can live in harmony and the delight of one-ness with one another and with our Father God—for the sake of His great and glorious Name.

---

1 Yevamot 13b.

2 Zechariah 8:19

3 Ephesians 2:14

Chukkat - חקת

Statute

Numbers 19:1–22:1; Judges 11:1–33;
John 3:14-21; 4:3–30

Themes of water, sin, life and death are interwoven in the *parasha* this week. The Israelites are nearing the end of their wilderness wanderings, and the deaths of Aaron and Miriam are recorded. They are honored as two of the three "good leaders" of Israel, along with Moses. However, just as their brother, they are destined not to enter the Promised Land.

It is of interest to note that after Miriam's death is recorded, the following verse states: *"And there was no water for the congregation…"* (20:2). The Sages of Israel considered that the Divine Well that accompanied the children of Israel and provided water in the desert was due to Miriam's qualities of praise and devotion to God. They concluded therefore that it dried up at her death.

The Mysterious Red Heifer

The first phrase in the opening verse can be translated: "*This is a basic statute of teaching that God has commanded…*" The Hebrew words *chukkat Torah* introduce the mysterious rite of purification in which the ashes of a perfect red heifer are a component. The term used in conjunction with this rite is "*an everlasting statute*" (19:10), indicating the seriousness and indispensability of the regulation and denoting its importance in God's eyes. The matter is thus worthy of our attention.

The specific purpose of the ritual is the restoration of purity after contact with a dead body. The preparation of the necessary ashes was conducted as follows:

> a) The priest sprinkled some of the blood of the slain heifer towards the entrance of the Sanctuary seven times, indicating the dedication of the procedure to God.
>
> b) While the carcass was being burnt, he threw cedar wood, hyssop and a scarlet cord into the flames, and then retired to cleanse himself.
>
> c) Someone who was ritually pure then collected the ashes and removed them to a specific place outside the camp where they were stored. They would be used in the purification ritual together with "living water" (*mai'yim chai'yim*—water from a natural source, e.g., rain water or water from a stream or well).

A person who came in contact with a dead body was ceremonially unclean for seven days (19:11) and could not enter the Temple. To be purified, he needed to be sprinkled with a mixture of the ashes of the heifer and living water on the third day and on the seventh day. Thereafter he could resume worship in the Temple.

There is a clear juxtaposition here of death and life. Verse nine adds the concept that the procedure is "*...a purification from sin*," thus making a connection with sin and death and highlighting the cleansing, redeeming property of the water.

The purification ceremony resulted in ritual cleansing of the person both physically and spiritually. The combination of living water, the blood of the heifer and the sacrificial ashes presents a picture of intimate relationship between the organic, transient, physical dimension and the eternal, spiritual, divine realm. Both aspects are perfectly combined in Yeshua the Messiah of God.

The efficacy of His atoning sacrifice and the power of His eternal life—represented by the blood He shed and the water of the living Word, both of which flowed from Him – provide purification from sin and death, and equip us for service under the Kingship of God.

The Third and the Seventh Days

Why did a person need to be sprinkled on the third and seventh days in order to be purified? Rabbi S.R. Hirsch in his inspiring commentary, *The Pentateuch*, offers a premise that ties in well with the interweaving of the physical and spiritual elements mentioned above. He points out that God created the material world on the third day and it was completely under His dominion. Man was created on the sixth day and God honored him by giving him mastery over the physical world.

However, on the seventh day, man is given the opportunity to rest from his creative labors in governing the earth and to honor His Creator by placing those powers once again under the Almighty's dominion. Just as God '*Sabbathed*' on the seventh day to focus upon and enjoy His creation, in turn man is exhorted to rest on the seventh day in order to focus upon and enjoy his God.

The Sin of Moses and the Waters of Meribah

We see another link between water and sin, when the sin of Moses and Aaron is mentioned twice in chapter 20. As a result of this transgression, they forfeit the honor of leading the Israelites into the Promised Land. The first reference is found in verses 12-13: *...ye believed not in Me, to sanctify Me in the eyes* *of the children of Israel*; and the second in verses 23-24: *...ye rebelled against My Word at the waters of Meribah.*

There has been much discussion and debate as to the nature of the sin that Moses and Aaron committed. Some commentators hold that Moses erred in losing patience and exhibiting anger before the people, when God Himself was not angry with them for requesting water. Others note that Moses asked, "Shall *we* bring you forth water?" rather than "Shall *God* bring you forth water?" This would have misled the people, suggesting that it was by Moses' and Aaron's own power that water would come forth from the rock. The most common view, however, is that Moses sinned when he *struck* the rock instead of *speaking* to it, as God had instructed.

Certainly it would have been a more impressive miracle for water to gush forth from the rock at Moses' spoken command rather than after he gave it a physical blow with his staff. The view of the renowned medieval commentator Rashi, as recorded by Nechama Leibowitz[1], suggests that the command to "*...speak ye unto the rock before their eyes*" (20:8) was intended to "open their eyes" – that is to give them increased spiritual insight and understanding. Rashi proposes that God's response to Moses was:

> Had you spoken to the rock to bring forth water I would have been sanctified in the eyes of the congregation, who would have argued [reasoned]: 'If this rock which can neither speak nor hear yet fulfils the word of the Omnipresent, how much more so [should] we.'

A unique opportunity was lost to honor the Name of God before the people, and thereby to inspire them to walk in greater love and obedience to Him and His Word, for their greater blessing. As his priests and witnesses, may our eyes be open to such opportunities in our journey with the Lord.

---

1 Nechama Leibowitz, *Studies in Bamidbar (Numbers), Chukkat.*

Balak - בלק
Balak

Numbers 22:2–25:9; Micah 5:6–6:8;
Jude

Although the *parasha* this week is named after Balak, it is more accurately the story of Balaam. The importance of Balaam's story is underscored in the Hebrew Scriptures. It is recorded in all three sections of the *Tanakh* (the Hebrew Bible) namely: the Torah, the Prophets (in Micah, the *haftarah* this week), and the Writings (in Nehemiah 13). It also is referred to numerous times in the *Brit Chadasha* (New Testament).

There are amazing connections between the beautiful *haftarah* reading from the prophet Micah and the Torah portion. In his time Micah denounced the corrupt, indulgent and luxurious lifestyle of many of the wealthy. He admonished all the people, no matter their status, to focus on what was significant and lasting in the light of eternity—their relationships with God and their fellow man.

Hear the Lord and Obey

In 6:4-5, Micah exhorts Israel to hear the Lord and to remember the *tzidkot Adonai*, God's righteous acts; His redemptive works that brought about their salvation, both physical and spiritual. Micah lists the examples of their deliverance from

Egypt and the repercussions of the plot against them that was spearheaded by Balak, the king of Moab, and Balaam, the famed soothsayer-prophet of Mesopotamia.

The Israelites had requested passage through Balak's land. In his unreasonable opposition to them, the king calls for Balaam, whose incantations and curses are known never to fail. He implores Balaam to curse the Israelites that he might overcome them. In effect, he is challenging the God of Abraham, Isaac and Jacob—the eternal King. In response, God intervenes and turns the curses into blessings.

We read in the fascinating account of Balaam that he did in fact hear from God, of whom he had presumably learned through his father Laban and distant cousin Jacob, (22:12). He resists, however, wanting to go his own way and God allows him to go. En route, however, the famous incident is recorded of his angry conversation with his donkey and his encounter with the angel. God may allow us to go ahead in our own designs and arrogance, contrary to His Word, but then He may "hem us in", narrowing our options until we are forced to hear Him.

The angel of the Lord says in verse 32: "*I have come to hinder you.*" Sometimes it is not people or circumstances that stand in our way, it is God Himself, working to get our attention! In verse 35, the angel echoes the very words God speaks to Balaam in verse 20: "*Only the word that I shall speak to you, that you shall speak*"—indicating that it is the Lord Himself who is speaking.

Curses become Blessings

When Balaam arrives at his destination Balak excitedly takes him to a succession of three "high places of sacrifice," the sites from which he anticipates his crippling curses will be pronounced upon Israel. To Balak's disappointment and chagrin, each time Balaam speaks forth blessings instead of curses, in accordance with God's will. Among the blessings—and in reiteration of the words proclaimed by God to Abraham in Genesis 12:3—Balaam proclaims a key element of Israel's destiny among the nations: "*May those who bless you be blessed and those who curse you be cursed*" (24:9b).

The first site Balak has planned is the "*high places of Baal*," the idol representing physical power and financial prosperity. Rather than cursing the Israelites in this respect, Balaam blesses their growth as a people and confirms that they are set apart for righteousness (23:9).

The second site is the "*field of Seers*." This represents intellectual and spiritual prowess. Can Balaam bring a curse here? He responds: "*God is with Israel and homage to the King is within him*" (23:21). It is not divination or magic that keeps Israel strong, only the presence of the King in their midst. He is their inspiration, their strength and their shield.

The third location is "*the peak of Pe'or*"—a place of lawless immorality and carnality. Pe'or was the seat of a sect of depraved sensuality that considered the human body on the same level as an animal, and thus nothing was cause for shame. Balaam cannot curse them from here either; instead he expresses his awe at the beauty and order of Israel's encampment:

> "*Mah tovu ohaleikha, Ya'akov, mishkenoteikha, Yisrael! How goodly are thy tents, O Jacob, Thy dwellings, O Israel!*" (24:5).

The same blessing serves as the opening proclamation of every synagogue service to this day.

Sin and Rebellion

At this point it seems that Balaam has sincerely repented and is honoring the Lord. However, his true colors are revealed, as we are told later in Numbers 31:16 (and confirmed by the Lord in

Revelation 2:14). He contrives a wicked plan and advises Balak to undermine the people of Israel through seduction and immorality.

Tragically, this is what befalls Israel when the idolatrous women of Moab and Midian lure them into sin through licentious Pe'oric sensuality. As a result 24,000 men die in a plague sent by God, as compared with 3,000 who died as a result of the sin of the Golden Calf. The plague is halted only when Aaron's grandson, Pinchas, rises up in zeal for the holiness of God, and thrusts through with a spear both Zimri, a prince of the tribe of Shimon, and Kosbi, a Midianite princess, who are blatantly and defiantly engaging in sexual intercourse before the Tabernacle of God.

Although God offers eternal blessing, His people come to ruin through immorality and rebellion. The Israelites find themselves in a cursed place where, due to the sin that separates them from His Presence, they are unable to receive or retain the blessing of God. Their only hope is to accept His gift of repentance, surrender to His perfect will, and return to Him in true humility of heart.

A Star and a Scepter

God's greatest righteous-saving act will be the in-breaking of Messiah, the Savior and Redeemer of the world, the eternal King of kings. This is referred to in Micah 5:2:

> *But you, O Bethlehem Ephratha, though you are least among the clans of Judah, from you shall come forth for Me one who is to be ruler in Israel, whose origin is from of old, from ancient days.*

This promise is uttered in one of the oracles of Balaam: "*I see him, but not now; I behold him, but not near—a star shall come out of Jacob, and a scepter shall rise out of Israel*" (Numbers

24:17). It is confirmed in Matthew 2:6, by the wise men from the East who follow the portentous star that signals the birth of the King of the Jews. They arrive in Bethlehem to worship the King and to present the Messiah with their three gifts of gold, frankincense and myrrh.

What do we bring our faithful, righteous God in return for His great gift? The prophet Micah declares that the Lord does not need countless animal sacrifices or rivers of oil to please Him; rather He has shown us what is good and what He requires of us:

> *To act justly, and to love chesed (kindness and covenant faithfulness), and to walk humbly with your God* (6:8).

Pinchas - פִּינְחָס

Phinehas

Numbers 25:10–30:1; 1 Kings 18:46–19:21;
John 2:12–25

Last week's parasha, *Balak*, concluded on a dramatic note. In the face of an outrageous act of immorality and idolatry that was a blatant profanation of the Name of God, Pinchas acts. Thousands were dying as the result of the plague; something had to be done. Where was Moses? In the past he always intervened and interceded if anything was out of order. Did the sheer monstrosity of the event paralyze him into passivity?

Another question is raised. Is a radical act like Pinchas' accepted as an ideal in the eyes of God? He obviously does not encourage random violence, even as a stand for 'right'. However, as we see in the first verse of this week's portion, God confirms that Pinchas' action is indeed righteous when He establishes a covenant of peace with him.

Active Peace

This covenant of peace recognizes that the outworking of true peace sometimes requires brave action. Tears and passive intention are not enough. Furthermore, it illustrates, as in the case of Pinchas, that peace is God's reward for righteous action and not an isolated end in itself. There is an inherent danger present when peace becomes an idol with the slogan: "Peace at any price." True and lasting peace cannot be achieved by means of any humanistic, man-made agenda established outside of the context of the Word and will of God.

The covenant also affirms that Pinchas' fearless deed is inspired by pure motives, for the sake of God's holy Name. As a result, God stops the plague and confers upon Pinchas and his descendents the honor of ongoing and permanent right to the position of High Priest. Pinchas was the son of Eleazar and the grandson of Aaron; however the fact of birth was not in itself sufficient to ensure an appointed place in the priesthood. The Lord knew that, in the tradition of Abraham, the pure, wholehearted zeal of Pinchas would be transferred to his sons and their sons after them.

One of the lessons this dramatic account teaches is that apathy is an enemy of the soul. It drains away enthusiasm in our service and devotion to God. If we sit idly by in spiritual passivity, then the spirit of the age can enter in—that self-centered freedom of expression that says, "*If it feels good, do it!*" Peoric self-indulgence takes precedence over the ideals and commandments of God's Word.

However, the question still remains in the account of Pinchas: Why did the Lord reward a seemingly violent act with peace? Rabbi A.L. Scheinbaum[1] offers some understanding. He recounts an analogy presented by one of the sages, Rabbi Chaim, who compares the situation to a homeowner who purchases a cat when his home is infested with mice. They both are aware of the problematic presence of the mice and want them removed one way or the other. What is the difference between the attitude of the owner of the home and the cat? The owner would be happy if no mouse disturbed his home at all, while the cat is eager to encounter and kill as many mice as possible!

We can assume that violence was far from 'natural' for Pinchas. The ultimate aim of the true godly "zealot" is to initiate peace and reconciliation—between man and God, and man and man. This is illustrated in Joshua chapter 22, where

Pinchas successfully mediates a disagreement between the tribes of Reuven, Gad and half of Manasseh and the rest of Israel. This incident is viewed by some rabbinic commentators as the time he truly steps forward as a leader and mediator of the covenant of peace with which he was entrusted.

The Appointment of Yehoshua / Joshua

Joshua had served Moses faithfully throughout the wilderness journey. He had always been at his side, assisting, watching, and learning all that the Lord was teaching Moses. He was the ideal disciple. Nevertheless, when the time came to appoint his successor, Moses didn't assume the obvious, but looked to the Lord to *set a man over the congregation* (27:16). Only He who truly knows "all flesh" is qualified to appoint a shepherd for His sheep (v.17). Immediately the Lord confirms the appointment of Joshua, *a man in whom is the Spirit* (v.18). He instructs Moses to lay his hand upon Joshua in the view of all the people and to honor him in their sight (v.19, 20).

Joshua's life bore witness to the fact that he would continue to lead the people in the Spirit of the Lord, according to the truth and instruction of His Torah, as Moshe before him. Change for the sake of change is generally ill advised. Major change is only necessary when something is out of order and not working correctly.

The ways of God established in His Word are eternal and not subject to compromise and alteration in order to suit the shifting whims and fancies of man. Yeshua (from the same Hebrew root as *Yehoshua*) is the Word made flesh, the Torah incarnate. We see in the gospels that His life and teaching uphold the Word given to Moshe. How could it be otherwise? That is who He is. To undermine, neglect or change any essentials of Torah would be in effect to undermine, neglect and diminish His own identity.

Zealous Peacemakers

The *haftarah* this week (1 Kings 18:46–19:21) connects the zeal of Pinchas and the zeal of Elijah. In very different circumstances, God met with and directed each one as to his future service in furthering His Kingdom in the earth. God saw that the burning desire of their hearts was to sanctify and honor His Name, and this brought blessing to the Father's heart.

We see in the *parasha* that Pinchas was the conveyor of God's covenant of peace. Similarly, in biblical and Jewish literature, the prophet Elijah—as the herald of Messiah—is esteemed as the reconciler and bringer of peace.

> *He will turn the hearts of parents to their children and the hearts of children to their parents*[2].

Whether rising up in action or retreating and seeking God's face, whether in the presence of fear or the lack thereof, each of us needs to have his or her heart turned in loving zeal and devotion to our Father God. He will be faithful to guide our steps by His Spirit, to encourage our hearts, and to enable us to walk forward for His glory in the covenant of peace in Messiah Yeshua, the *Sar Shalom*—the Prince of Peace, the ultimate Reconciler.

---

[1] Rabbi A.I. Scheinbaum, *Peninim on the Torah*, 274.

[2] Malachi 4:6

Mattot - מטות

Tribes

Numbers 30:2–32:42; Jeremiah 1:1–2:3
Philippians 2:1–16a

The Power of Words

The *parasha* opens with a perplexing reference to vows and oaths and certain conditions pertaining thereto. In biblical times these were more clearly defined and in effect than in recent history. There are nevertheless, as in every passage of Scripture, important principles to be gleaned.

The Hebrew terms clarify the difference between a vow, *neder* and an oath, *shvu'ah*. The shvu'ah indicates that the responsibility and the consequences are incumbent upon the one who utters it, as in the case of Shimei[1]. The neder is usually a proclamation in the context of personal commitment to the Lord, as in a Nazarite vow. The neder once spoken, in the same manner as a curse, seems to have an inherent power and can have repercussions on others apart from the one making the vow. A vow, therefore, as well as responsibility carries with it some danger.

Midrash Rabbah[2] records:

> Four made vows; two lost and two profited. Yisrael and Hannah profited; Yiftach [Jephthah] and Jacob vowed and lost.

Jephthah, in his arrogant self-confidence, made a rash and irresponsible vow that, sadly, affected his daughter's life[3]. Jacob innocently made a thoughtless vow to Laban[4] that resulted in the untimely death of Rachel.

This is a compelling reminder of the power of words. They can and do affect life—our own and that of others. They can bring about negative, even deadly, results or they can be life-giving and bear forgiveness and peace. This adds impetus to the counsel of James:

> *But above all, my brethren, do not swear, either by heaven or by earth or with any other oath, but let your yes be yes and your no be no, that you may not fall under condemnation* (5:12).

Sticks and Branches?

The Hebrew words most commonly used in the Bible to designate *tribe*, as in the *tribes* of Israel, are *shevet* and *mateh*. The latter is the name of our parasha, in the plural form—*Mattot*. Both these words have the primary meanings of staff, stick, rod (which also carry connotations of authority) and, by extension, branch. This last meaning emphasizes that each tribe is a branch of the larger whole. Each has its unique role to play in fulfilling the mission of the entire nation. If a branch breaks away "to do its own thing" it will surely wither and die[5]. In addition the tree itself will be weakened. It is made clear in the Biblical narrative that the chief causes of Israel breaking away from the source of life, God Himself, were idol worship and immorality.

God's people were seduced into the worship of the idol Peor and were thereby weakened morally and spiritually. Their true enemy, Balak, king of Midian, inspired by the false prophet Balaam, had conspired towards Israel's moral and spiritual destruction. As God's people, we can be weakened and even destroyed physically, but if we stand upright spiritually and persist in faithfulness, bound to God, He remains ever-constant and our lives rest secure in Him for eternity. Yeshua Himself said:

> *"I am the vine, you are the branches. He who abides in me, and I in him, he it is that bears much fruit, for apart from me you can do nothing [of lasting worth]. If a man does not abide in me, he is cast forth as a branch and withers; and the branches are gathered, thrown into the fire and burned."*[6]

If one's moral and spiritual integrity are consistently weakened, and one is torn away from the Vine, or broken as a branch from the tree of Life, without repentance one faces the consequences of death and despair.

War Against Evil

Though Moses' commands in the war against Midian may seem merciless, the power of evil had to be broken leaving no room for its fatal influences. We read that Balaam was killed in the battle (31:8). He was the catalyst for the evil and impurity, and *Moshe* (Moses), who represented the holiness and purity of God, defeated him. This war was the last deed Moshe was called to perform for God before he died, highlighting its significance.

The portion opens with the verse: *And Moshe spoke: This is the word that the Lord has commanded.* We can recall that when God first summoned Moshe to speak on His behalf to Pharoah, he shrank from the task saying, "Who am I…?" The Lord assured him, "*Certainly, I will be with you*"[7]. They would go *together*. Moshe may have felt that God in His mighty power could do supernaturally all that was needed to rescue His people from Egypt. However, as God proceeded to illustrate, although He indeed is the Redeemer He invites and indeed requires His servants to work together with Him in the earth.

Today the evils of immorality and idolatry have been let loose like a flood. We may think, "Who am I that I should oppose the lies and conspiracy of the 'snake'—the enemy of our souls—and speak the truth of the Word of God?" The Lord has clearly shown that our words and deeds on His behalf are vital in the outworking of His Divine plan. This should be our highest goal, in answer to His call: to be a vessel for the expression of His truth and will wherever He places us, and to encourage one another to work together as branches of the same holy Vine, "*to the glory of God the Father.*"[8]

---

[1] 1 Kings 2:36-44

[2] Genesis 70:3

[3] Judges11:30-31

[4] Genesis 31:33

[5] cf. Romans 11

[6] John 15:5,6

[7] Exodus 3:12

[8] Philippians 2:11

Massei - מסעי

Journeys

Numbers 33:1–36:13; Jeremiah 2:4–28, 3:4, 4:1–2;
1 John 1:5–2:6

This final portion of the book of Numbers, *B'midbar*, begins with an overview of the journey of the Israelites through the wilderness. On reading chapter 33 one is struck by the repetition of the words "they journeyed" and "they camped." These words are reiterated forty-two times in the Torah.

In Hebrew they are *va'yissu* and *va'yachanu* which combined and repeated a number of times beat out a rhythm reminiscent of a chugging locomotive. This imparts the sensation of movement, of journeying. At relevant points the forward movement stops suddenly, as if the train has arrived at a station, and something of importance is drawn to one's attention. For example, upon the arrival at Elim (33:9) twelve springs of water and seventy palm trees are noted.

The Journey of Life

Every word, indeed every letter, of the Scriptures is God-breathed[1] and carries life and meaning. Thus, as the sages of old and Bible scholars through the centuries have discovered, every detail is important and contains layer upon layer of meaning, all documented and woven together by the Master Craftsman. As we study, and search, and wrestle with the biblical text, our efforts are rewarded when these wondrous layers are revealed—a piece here, or a glimpse there.

What of the details described in 33:9—twelve springs of water and seventy palm trees? Certainly there are various possible meanings. One possibility harmonizes with the theme of the *parasha* and the whole book of Numbers, and in fact with the whole Torah: that of a journey, our life journey. The clue is the number 70, which correlates with a life span of "*threescore years and ten*"[2]. The number 12, in relation to this, corresponds with the months in a year. Each year marks a milestone in our life's journey. It is *this* journey that is of ultimate importance in the eyes of our Father in heaven.

How do we walk through the cycle of our years according to His Word and direction? Like any successful journey, it requires effort, preparation, focused attention and, sometimes, a sacrifice of our personal comfort. Also required are rest stops, oases, places of refreshment, and reorientation.

The Annual Cycle

The Cycle of Life ties in with another theme that is woven through God's Word: the annual Festival Cycle. Again we find a repetitive pattern of words, "*on the...day*" and "*unto the Lord*", which also captures the cadence of motion. However, it is more like a steady walk than a train-ride. This is the measured rhythm of time and seasons—God's cycle of the year. The concept and description of this "walk" through each year is replete with meaningful details that demand our attention.

The purpose of stops on a journey is for refreshment. Also of great importance is the need to look back, to study and analyze the ups and downs, to learn from our mistakes in order that the next stage of the journey will be smoother and more meaningful. We can view each of the *Mo'adim* ("Appointed Times" of the Lord, the annual Festivals) as such a stop. We stop and 'camp' for a time to meet with God in a special way.

Each 'camp-site' has its unique characteristics and important lessons that the Lord desires to impress upon us. Every Feast, in its turn, affords an opportunity to look back, to reflect upon and to learn from the last stage of our journey. We can then move forward, with the Lord's guidance, into the next stage with greater wisdom, hope and anticipation. He is our Guide, just as in the wilderness account. He is our Protector and our Provider as He leads us through life in His paths of righteousness[3].

The Daughters of Zeloph'ehad

Both *Massei,* and the journey *B'midbar*, end with a reference to Zelophehad's five daughters. Our focus returns to *Pinchas*, where their story is told in chapter 27:1–11. Why is this issue of such importance that it has the honor of closing this fourth book of the Torah?

The brave and righteous stand of these women transformed the laws of inheritance amongst the people of Israel. Whereas previously only sons could inherit from their father, now daughters and women were also entitled to an inheritance. The Talmud records that Zelophehad's daughters were regarded by the Sages as: "wise women, learned women [in the Word], righteous women"[4]. They knew that: "He who created the world extends His love to *all* His children. His tender mercies are over all His works."

The daughters' focus, however, was not on themselves; their motivation was to secure and uphold the good name of their father (27:4). Also, in contrast with bad report of the ten spies, they recognized that the Land promised by God was "*good and spacious.*" It was Israel's inheritance from their loving Father in heaven (26:53) and they desired to gratefully receive their portion. May we be equally committed to honoring our Father's Name.

Chazak, chazak, ve'nitchazek!
Be strong, be strong, and let us strengthen one another!

---

1 Cf. Paul's affirmation in 2 Timothy 3:16.

2 Psalm 90:10

3 Psalm 23:3

4 Bava Batra 119b

DEUTERONOMY

DEVARIM - דברים

The Land - Place of Promise

Devarim—Deuteronomy, the last of the five books of the Torah, is the book Yeshua most often quoted. The portions of the book are rich and significant and address many of the key concepts and themes of the whole Torah, indeed of the whole Word of God.

Devarim is divided into four sections: three are discourses of Moses to the people and the fourth describes his last days and includes a Song and a Blessing. As recorded in Jewish tradition, Moses took thirty-six days to deliver this series of discourses (from 1 Shevat through 6 Adar). It comprises an intensive course of study in preparation for entering the Land of Promise.

The Hebrew noun *banim* (children) can also be read *bonim* (builders). Thus Isaiah 54:13 can be rendered:

> *And all your children/builders shall be taught of the* LORD, *and great shall be the peace of your children/builders.*

In our times God is using His children as builders in the restoration of His Land, with Zion at its heart. They are each precious in His sight and appear to Him as rare and sparkling jewels in the crown that is being prepared wherewith to adorn the King of kings. These builders are not always clearly discernible to the natural eye, but the Lord has many children/ builders in the Land and also spread abroad to the four corners of the earth.

As His children, we are privileged to be among those in this generation who are called to participate in His building up of Israel. Every small physical deed and action, every heartfelt prayer, every tear shed, every joy celebrated by each "builder" is a part of His plan for the restoration and rebuilding of Zion, to the end that His glory might be revealed in all the earth.

> *You will arise and have pity on Zion; it is the time to favor her; the appointed time has come. For your servants hold her stones dear and have pity on her dust. Nations will fear the name of the Lord, and all the kings of the earth will fear your glory. For when the Lord builds up Zion; He appears in His glory…* (Psalm 102:13-17).

Devarim - דברים
Words

Deuteronomy 1:1–3:22; Isaiah 1:1–27;
1Timothy 3:1–7

The original name of this book of the Torah was *Mishneh Torah* (Repetition of the Torah). Greek-speaking Jews translated it as *Deuteronomion* (Second Law), which was adopted in Latin as *Deuteronomium,* and thus into English as *Deuteronomy.* The present Hebrew name, *Devarim,* was taken from the opening phrase: *Eleh ha'devarim... These are the words...* (1:1).[1]

The emphasis on repetition indicates that one of the main purposes of the book of Deuteronomy is to encourage us to review what has gone before. Throughout our lives we are continually learning; however we also have a strong tendency to forget! Repetition and revision are important tools in helping us retain what we have learnt.

Devarim is the fifth and last of the Five Books of Moses. Distilled within it is the teaching of the previous books, with the primary focus on *how to live* as God's people. At the same time, seventy percent of the instructions given here by Moses are entirely new. He demonstrates for us that the great truths of God's Torah need to be constantly learned anew for they always yield ever-expanding, deeper and richer insights. A good teacher prepares his students for future needs not yet experienced while reinforcing the lessons of the past.

New Life in the Promised Land

Moses is aware that this is his last opportunity personally to share God's Word with the people of Israel before his death; before they embark on the final stage of their journey into the Promised Land and a completely new life.

They are about to transition from life as a single community, one that is daily dependent on God's power, protection and provision, to a more individualized, private lifestyle. They will need to settle down and provide for themselves. The need then will be even greater to remember their God and to call upon Him. They also will need to remember their united calling as a people—to live as a *kingdom of priests and a holy nation*[2]. Thus Moses' teaching, on how to do this according to God's will and instruction, takes on heightened significance.

The Land they are entering is an inheritance from their Father God, and it will be the place of their maturing and developing as a nation. Their conception and formation in the womb, as it were, occurred with Abraham, Isaac and Jacob. They suffered their birth pangs in Egypt and were delivered through the waters of *Yam Suf* (the Red or Reed Sea). They learnt to walk and grow as a child in the wilderness. Now they have reached *Bar Mitzvah*—the age of independent accountability.

Through their teacher Moses, their Father bestows upon them His loving words of instruction and preparation for this important step into the future. God's greatest desire as a loving Father is that they move into mature, fulfilled adulthood as a nation; that they live a life that will be filled with wisdom, peace and His blessing. Thus Moses warns them repeatedly to remember the mighty revelations of their God, and not to be led astray from His Word by turning to idol worship with its evils and aberrations. They are facing the great temptations and choices of young adulthood.

Review of the Journey

Moses took thirty-six days to deliver this final series of teachings. An intensive course of study.

This week we read the first of his three discourses, which is a history lesson —a review of the Israelites' journey from *Horeb* (Mount Sinai) to *Kadesh Barnea.* We are informed in verse 2 that it is *"eleven days' journey"* between these two points. Eleven days were extended to forty years!

Moses is trying to impress upon this new generation the need to review the sins and weaknesses that caused the *dor ha'midbar* (the wilderness generation) to forfeit their right to enter the Land. Would they immediately have entered in, they would not have been prepared and would have defiled the Land in their ignorance. Therefore, they needed to remain under God's constant care and training as children before they could accept and face responsibility. On their long and arduous journey towards accountability, the Israelites experienced God's faithful and tender care. They saw,

> *... how the LORD your God bore you, as a man bears his son, all the way that you went until you came to this place* (1:31).

Lessons on the Way

The message from God to His people is as fresh to us today as it was then. These are a few significant lessons that emerge from Moses' discourse:

- *Be grateful, and do not murmur and complain* (1:27).

  Murmuring is a sign of unbelief and ingratitude for the goodness of God's provision in the past. As we saw demonstrated with the wilderness generation, this leads to a hardening of heart that hinders the blessing of God and prevents the future good He has planned.

- *Obey God's Word, and do not rebel* (1:43).

  When we rebel against God's commands and act presumptuously in our own strength, we forfeit His presence and blessing and are doomed to ultimate failure.

- *Defend yourselves, but do not contend [against other nations]* (2:5).

  Rabbi S.R. Hirsch comments on this verse:

  > All the nations, not only Israel, are under God's Providential rule, and have had their territories assigned to them … Israel must confine his ambitions to the one Land Divinely assigned to him at the very beginning of his being as a family [i.e. with Abraham].[3]

  Every nation must defend itself against enemy attack. However, the foundation of Israel's security, as well as ours individually, is not primarily our physical location but the unfailing love of the One who has proved to be mighty, true and faithful.

- *Do not be afraid.*

  Moses concludes this portion with a repetition of the assurance proclaimed in the first paragraph (1:30):

  "Ye shall not fear; for the Lord your God, He it is that fights for you!" (3:22).

  When we stand in faithfulness and trust we will see the salvation of our God and witness that the Lord indeed is good. We need have no fear of men or circumstances. As we stand in 'fear' of God we see that it is He who fights for us.

---

1 Dr.J.H.Hertz, *Pentateuch and Haftorahs*, 735.

2 Exodus 19:6

3 Rabbi S.R. Hirsch, *The Pentateuch*, 743.

Va'etchanan - ואתחנן

And I Besought

Deuteronomy 3:23–7:11; Isaiah 40:1–26;
Luke 4:1–13

> *And I besought the* Lord *at that time: "O Lord God, You have begun to give Your servant insight into Your greatness and Your mighty hand"* (3:23).

This is an intense and deeply emotional moment for Moses. He strongly desires to cross over into the Promised Land with his people. He knows it is *there* that the purposes of God will be worked out. From there—His Land—God will show His greatness, will reveal His "mighty hand" to all peoples, and will establish His Kingdom on earth. Moses confesses, at the same time, that as great as the vision and insights are that the Lord is revealing, they are only the first glimmerings of the understanding of His greatness and of how majestic and powerful are His purposes.

Moses exhibits the qualities of true leadership when he humbly and openly shares with the people God's denial of his request. He honors the appointment of Joshua in his stead and encourages and strengthens the new leader.

Then God, in His love for His servant Moses, tells him to ascend Pisgah, a high mountain in the area, and from there graciously affords him a glorious view of all the Land of promise. It was a supernatural view—one which I believe included a prophetic vision; a revelation of what would transpire in the future outworking of God's mighty redemptive plan. The plan that is centered on His Land, His people, and the place where He chooses to set His Name forever, Mount Zion in Jerusalem[1].

This deeper understanding of God's purposes for this people in this Land gives added impetus to Moses' gathering of the Israelites and the delivery of his final discourses. These encapsulate the words and teachings of their Father in heaven, who desires to prepare His children to face the challenges of the great mission that lay ahead.

Sh'ma Yisrael - Hear O Israel!

Moses knew that the one indispensable condition upon which the future victory and prosperity of the people depended was obedience to the will of God as expressed in His Word. He urgently proclaims:

> *And now, O Israel, hear the statutes and ordinances I am teaching you today ... so that you may live and possess the Land* (4:1).

These words of Torah mean life to His people.

> *Keep hold of [God's Word of] instruction, do not let go; guard her for she is your life.*[2]

In vital affirmation of this, Yeshua, the Word-made-flesh, proclaims:

> "*... the words that I have spoken to you are spirit and life!*" [3]

And He promises in Luke 6:47, "*Every one who comes to me and hears my words and does them ...*" will remain unshaken in the Kingdom of God. That person will be like a house built on rock, for his life is established on the foundation of truth. Hearing God's Word with yielded hearts, and acting upon it in an attitude of grateful and willing obedience, brings blessing, security and life.

When we truly hear Him our response involves every aspect of our life. This is highlighted in the portion by the declaration of Moses that has become the constant affirmation of faith of the Jewish people, morning and evening:

> *Sh'ma Yisrael—Hear O Israel—the Lord our God, the Lord is One. And you shall love the Lord your God with all your heart, and with all your soul, and with all your might …* (6:4-9).

The Big Ten

The *Sh'ma* underscores the unity and the love of God. Inextricably linked with it is the Decalogue, or Ten Commandments, also found in this *parasha.*

The ten words (*devarim*) spoken by God at Sinai were engraved on stone by the "finger" or Spirit of God[4] —the same Spirit who engraves the Word on our hearts[5]. The first five 'words' relate to one's conduct towards God, and the second five, to one's conduct towards one's fellow man. These unchanging statutes, literally "set in stone," are the fundamental principles of the Torah and are at the very heart of God's covenant with His people. They are the basis of the righteous, peaceful and joy-filled life incarnated in Yeshua—the abundant and eternal life in the Spirit for which He created us.

In order to aim towards this goal, Moses exhorts the people to "*fear the Lord your God*" and "*teach [His Word] to your children*" (4:10).

In Hebraic understanding *yi'rat Adonai* (fear of the Lord) is not a product of the emotions, but a reverential and loving attitude towards our heavenly Father that is taught and learned. *Learn to fear God, your God.*[6]

The word *lamad* (learn) connotes study *and* practice. Yeshua taught and demonstrated, in true humble obedience, that to be a disciple requires the constant growth of one's knowledge of God through study of His Word and by putting His instructions into practice. In His grace, and by the enabling of the Holy Spirit, our teaching and the modeling of our lives will pass on the valuable lesson of "fear of God" to the next generation.

Comfort Ye My People

The *haftarah* (prophetic reading) this week is Isaiah 40:1–26. It is the first of seven *Haftarot* of Consolation that follow the day of fasting, *Tisha b'Av* (9 Av). Many tragic events in Jewish history occurred on *Tisha b'Av*, including the destruction of the first and the second Holy Temples in Jerusalem.

Tens of thousands of Christians worldwide have found that the Spirit of the Lord has formed "a highway in their heart" to His holy Mount Zion. He has impressed upon them the vital calling of compassion and comfort. "*Comfort ye My people!*" *says the LORD* (40:1).

Throughout the Scriptures we see that, together with His revelation of power, the Lord always extends gentle tenderness to His people as a *shepherd that feeds His flock, and gathers the lambs in His arms and carries them in His bosom* (v.11).

Israel desperately needs the unwavering message of encouragement, hope and assurance of the unfailing purposes of God for His land and people. His promises do not fail. His love is eternal. The confirmation of this is relayed in verse 8:

> *The grass withers and the flowers fade; but the Word of our God shall stand forever.*

We can proclaim good news to Zion and glad tidings to Jerusalem and say to the cities of Judah: *Behold your God!* (40:9). He is with you and has not forsaken you. He is coming as the

"Mighty One" when His strong right arm will rule for Him and His recompense will be with Him (40:10).

He will redeem in full the cruelty and persecution that have been waged against His people and will restore their inheritance as in former days. Then, as promised by the prophet Zechariah, all the fast days of mourning *shall be to the house of Judah seasons of joy and gladness, and cheerful feasts; therefore love truth and peace* (8:19).

We can look up and lift our eyes (Isaiah 40:26) for our Redeemer draws nigh. The glory of the Lord shall be revealed in Jerusalem, and all flesh shall see it together. It shall be so, *for the mouth of the LORD has spoken it* (40:5).

---

1 See Deuteronomy12:11; Nehemiah 1:9; Isaiah 18:7

2 Proverbs 4:13

3 John 6:63

4 Exodus 31:18

5 Jeremiah 31:33

6 Deuteronomy 31:13

Ekev - עקב

Because

Deuteronomy 7:12–11:25; Isaiah 49:14–51:3;
James 5:7–11

> *It will come to pass, because of (ekev) your hearing these social ordinances (mishpatim) and carrying them out with care, that the* LORD *your God will keep for you the covenant (brit) and lovingkindness (chesed) that He swore to your fathers* (7:12).

The name of this week's portion, *Ekev*, bears comparison with the Hebrew word for *heel*. In the light of the context, we could say that the blessings of God enumerated in the ensuing verses follow on the 'heels' of our obedience.

As we willingly heed and obey His commandments, statutes and ordinances, our focus should not be on the rewards to be reaped; rather our joy should stem from hearing the Word of the Lord and wholeheartedly applying it to our lives for His glory. As loving children, we do this in order to please our Father in heaven. Then He assures us His blessings will follow.

Mishpatim - Social Ordinances

Last week we addressed the *chukim* (statutes) of God, which are exemplified in the Ten Words (Commandments) that are "set in stone" and inviolable for all time. Amongst them are three that, according to the Sages of Israel, a believer in God should not violate even under threat of death: idolatry, murder, and sexual immorality.

Indulgence in these particular sins leads to a form of death in and of itself.

- Turning to idolatry is a choice to remove oneself from the presence of the One true God, which is spiritual death.
- Hatred, of which murder in one form or another is a by-product, leads to moral death.
- Sexual immorality hardens the heart and leads to emotional death.

All three can overlap in significant ways and, unless truly repented of, lead ultimately to the eternal death of total separation from the holy God, the very Source of life.

Moses now proceeds with his second discourse to *adat Yisrael* (the congregation of Israel). The *mishpatim* referred to in verse twelve are commandments that relate specifically to the community. They address various aspects concerning the spiritual and physical lives of the individuals within it.

All of Creation contains inbuilt systems that operate in harmony with one another in order for life to function within the framework of the Creator's blessing. We see evidence of this in the natural order. When man interferes with or neglects to follow God's laws of nature, the result is destruction and disaster, which bring curses such as disease, poverty and starvation in their wake.

When His laws of nature are honored and man "takes care of the Garden" with which he has been entrusted, by investing his time, energy and expertise in studying and working within the God-ordained system, then harmony, blessing and prosperity flow forth.

Likewise, when people live in accord with their Creator's spiritual and relational laws, which foster right relationship with Him and with one another, they are blessed with harmony, peace and prosperity—as a community, as families, and individually.

Our Daily Bread

> *He fed you with manna ... that He might make you know that man does not live by bread alone, but that man lives by everything that proceeds out of the mouth of the Lord* (8:3).

Bread is a symbol of daily nourishment. It is also a visual illustration of the intelligence of man in creating sustenance for himself. Manna, on the other hand, is provided by God alone, without human effort or achievement. Manna reminds us that there is another dimension of supernatural provision, whereby God Himself sustains life. If we fail to acknowledge God's supreme control of the Universe, the same creative human power that produces bread will produce idolatry. It will result in humanistic worship of man in place of God, and will lead to the lawlessness (or Torah-lessness) that breeds ever-increasing immorality and violence.

Devarim 8:3 is the scripture quoted by Yeshua[1] to rebuff Satan's challenge in the wilderness that He turn stones into bread. This was as much a temptation to prove that He was the Divine Son as to ease His hunger. By His response, Yeshua affirms that life's fulfillment and sustenance is found in the Word of God. He is that Word-incarnate, the Life-giver, and He is not obliged to prove anything to the evil one.

Perhaps as a daily reminder of the sovereignty of God over all life, the injunction to "give thanks" for a meal is given in this parasha:

> *When you eat and are satisfied, then bless the* Lord, *your God* (8:10).

The intention of this offering of blessing to the Lord exceeds that of expressing gratitude for the meal just eaten. It also reminds us to rely upon God alone for our very existence, and to look to Him for the strength and ability to accomplish all He has called us to in this life.

Note that Deuteronomy 8:10 commands a blessing *after* a meal. Yeshua also gave thanks *before* the meal—honoring a custom instituted as an additional blessing by the Pharisees. To this day devout Jews bless God both before and after meals.

Every meal with bread is preceded by the blessing:

> *Barukh Atah Adonai Eloheinu, Melekh ha'Olam, ha'motzi lechem min ha'aretz.*
>
> Blessed are You O LORD our God, King of the Universe, who brings forth bread from the earth.

It is a great reminder that every piece of bread we eat, in fact our daily sustenance and strength, should be appreciated as a gift of God's goodness and gracious provision.

Israel's Comfort

This week's *haftarah* reading is the second "Haftarah of Consolation." Isaiah's message brings a word of comfort and hope to Israel in the midst of her suffering and distress. In dark times, when it seems as though the Lord has not heard her cry, Israel is comforted to know that even if it were possible for a nursing mother to forget her infant, the Lord will never forget His covenant people.

As a sign of His loving faithfulness, the Lord's beckoning hand will be raised as a signal to the nations. In response, many peoples will aid the return of Zion's scattered children by tenderly carrying them back to their land (verse 22). This will be an indication of the Lord's initiative in rebuilding and restoring Zion. Praise God that we are witnessing and experiencing this in our lifetime.

The *haftarah* this week contains a memorable verse:

> *Behold - see! - I have engraved thee upon the palms of My hands* (49:16).

It echoes Zechariah's remarkable prophecy of a coming time when, the Lord says:

> *I will pour out on the house of David and the inhabitants of Jerusalem a spirit of compassion and supplication, so that, when they look on [behold] him whom they have pierced, they shall mourn for him, as one mourns for an only child, and weep bitterly over him, as one weeps over a first-born* (12:10).

The theme of the suffering Messiah continues in Isaiah 50:6-7, where the prophet describes the one who sets his face like a flint, gives His back to the smiters, and does not shrink back from the shame. Yeshua endured all the suffering for the *joy that was set before Him,* and He is now *seated at the right hand of the throne of God*[2]. From there, as Zechariah prophesies in chapter 12:9, He will execute judgment on *all the nations that come against Jerusalem.*

Isaiah exhorts us to trust in the name of the Lord, and to wait upon our God (50:10). The God of Israel will redeem and He will reign!

Today we can behold and see that, even in the face of the relentless hatred and the unceasing vicious onslaught of the enemy, the deserted *waste places* of Zion are flourishing like the *garden of the Lord.*

We are indeed privileged to witness the first sure glimmerings of the final great redemption, and we can hope and trust that in ever-increasing measure, joy and gladness, *thanksgiving and the sound of melody* will be found in Zion (51:3).

---

[1] Luke 4:4

[2] Hebrews 12:2

Re'eh - ראה

Behold

Deuteronomy 11:26–16:17; Isaiah 54:11–55:5;
John 7:37–52

The Hebrew name of this *parasha* is the verb *re'eh* (behold). A form of the same word is used by Jeremiah when he says:

> *This is what the* Lord *says: "Stand at the crossroads and look (re'u), ask for the ancient paths, ask where the good way is, and walk in it, and you will find rest for your souls"* (6:16).

The biblical narrative in this final book of Torah, *Devarim*, describes the children of Israel at the "crossroads" of their wilderness journey. They are instructed by Moses, their teacher and leader, on the "good way" to follow once they enter the Land promised them by God.

The Choice is Ours

Via the gift of free will, God has placed the choice completely in the hands of mankind as to whether our future will be one of blessing or of curse. We see this clearly illustrated in the *parasha*. God gives His people the map and destination for their expedition through the wilderness, which represents the journey of every life. This includes: clear directions for the path to take, specific instructions on how best to cope with the conditions and to stay healthy on the journey, the dangers and pitfalls to avoid, and how to gain the most pleasure and enjoyment along the way.

The critical choices we must make at the crossroads of God are first, whether to continue on His path or not, and second, whether to follow His directions or not. One might set out on His path with good intentions, as did the Israelites, but soon discover that it is not a one-time choice. When Moses says, "*Behold! See! I am setting before you today blessing and curse*'" (11:26), it means *every* day. Every straying step from God's "*good way*," every act of disobedience unless repented of, will ultimately lead to death instead of life, to curse instead of blessing.

After their arrival in the Promised Land the people of Israel view the two prominent hills of Mount Gerizim and Mount Eibal. Gerizim is green and fertile, filled with fruit-bearing flora. A little further north, and somewhat higher, Mount Eibal is brown, steep, and barren of growth. They present a perfect object lesson and a vivid picture of blessing and curse, and can still be seen to this day in the region of Samaria in Israel.

Both hills stand in the same soil, receive the same rainfall and dew, and the same winds blow over each. Yet one is stark and devoid of growth and the other is filled with life and vegetation. This reminds us of the fact that external circumstances do not determine our blessings, or lack thereof. What counts is how we react to them. The choice is continually ours as to which path to take, which moral choices to make, and which guidelines to follow. Our choices determine which mount will symbolize our future—Gerizim or Eibal?

Be Altogether Joyful!

An important issue addressed by Moshe in this discourse is the injunction regarding giving to the Levites (who are without inheritance in the Land), to the poor, and to the widows and orphans.

True *tzedakah*, charity, is a combination of heart and action. True love of the Lord and of one's neighbor is evidenced in deeds that express active caring, one to another and in the context of community.

We learn from this *parasha* that righteous charitable giving is also connected with the seasons of joy—i.e., the appointed Feasts of the Lord. This is especially a focus on the three annual pilgrimage festivals mentioned in chapter 16: Passover (*Pesach*), Pentecost (*Shavu'ot*) and Tabernacles (*Sukkot*).

These are times set apart to rejoice before the Lord with your families, your servants, the spiritual leaders, and even with strangers and the poor—indeed all who are *in the midst of thee* (16:11). Why does the Lord command that we remember to give to the needy on these occasions? In order that we may receive His blessing.

> *Because the Lord your God shall bless you in all your increase, and in all the work of your hands, and you shall be altogether joyful!"* (16:15b).

Third Haftarah of Consolation - Hope

This third "*Haftara*h of Consolation" is Isaiah's call of hope to Jerusalem, which is afflicted and not comforted. It is a proclamation of assurance that the Lord is indeed building Zion in beauty and for His glory.

He is laying her foundations with sapphires as the base of His throne, described in Ezekiel's vision:

> *And above the firmament over their heads there was the likeness of a throne, in appearance like sapphire* (1:26).

And He is setting her walls and borders with radiant and colorful precious stones:

> *And I will make thy windows of agates, and thy gates of carbuncles, and all thy borders of pleasant stones.*[1]

While the God of Abraham, Isaac and Jacob calls and establishes His children-builders in their Land, the enemy of God gathers hate-driven forces against them, aiming for their destruction. But the Lord says: "*Whosoever shall gather together against thee shall fall because of thee ... No weapon that is formed against thee shall prosper*" (54:15,17a).

He promises His workers that: "*Their reward is from Me*" (54:17b).

It was at the climactic water-pouring ceremony on the seventh and last day of the joyous Feast of Tabernacles, when Yeshua issued the dramatic call:

> *If any one thirsts, let him come to Me and drink.*[2]

This connects powerfully with chapter fifty-five of the *haftarah,* where Isaiah invites everyone to come and partake of life-giving waters, of wine that gladdens the heart, and of milk that nourishes—the Living Word of God.

We are reminded that any 'building' we do outside of God's Kingdom purposes, as described in His Word, will fail to satisfy the soul. We were created for the righteous and holy endeavors prepared by our loving Father for each of His children from the beginning of time; endeavors that contribute to the unfolding of His progressive plan of redemption in the earth.

Let us be strong therefore and build—that the Almighty's glory might be established in all the earth and that many may come up to Zion, the city of our King, and learn of His ways and be comforted in Jerusalem.

---

[1] Isaiah 54:12

[2] John 7:37

Shoftim - שופטים

Judges

Deuteronomy 16:18–21:9; Isaiah 51:12–52:12;
Hebrews 10:28–31

In Scripture the qualities of truth (*emet*) and loving-kindness (*chesed*) very often are linked. This is a reminder that truth must be tempered with love. Paul's well-known exhortation in Ephesians 4:15 is a clear example: *Speaking the truth (emet) in love (chesed), we are to grow up in every way into him who is the head, into Messiah …*

The Psalmist also emphasizes this connection in 26:3 and 40:10-11. As well as in 138:2, which reads:

> *I bow down toward Thy holy temple and give thanks to Thy name for Thy steadfast love (chesed) and Thy truth (emet); for Thou hast exalted above everything Thy name and Thy word.*

Similarly, the concept of justice (*tzedek*) is often linked with compassion or mercy (*rachamim*). Consider Psalm 89:14, *Justice* (*tzedek*) *and judgment are the habitation of Thy throne: mercy* (*rachamim*) *and truth shall go before Thy face.*

Yeshua addresses the corrupt leaders of His time and chastises them for forgetting *…the weightier matters of the Law: justice* (*tzedek*) *and mercy* (*rachamim*) *and faith.*[1]

In a similar vein, two striking passages from the prophets, Hosea 2:19 and Micah 6:8, relate to God's covenant of love with us and our response of "doing" justice and loving kindness.

Tzedek, Tzedek!

The *parasha* opens with the verse:

> *Shoftim ve'shotrim (judges and officials) you shall appoint at all your gates ... and they shall judge the people with righteous judgment (mishpat tzedek)* (16:18).

The concept of justice is doubly stressed in 16:20,

> *Tzedek, tzedek tirdof - Justice, justice shalt thou pursue, that thou mayest live.*

The emphatic repetition and the context indicate that this is a keynote of God's teaching. Justice affects life. This theme is amplified throughout the Bible to instill the priority of social righteousness, which involves every individual and community as well as every nation. Righteous justice is the foundation of God's Kingdom rule, as we see expressed in Psalm 89: *Justice and judgment are the habitation of Thy throne.*

The basis of God's justice is the equal value of every human life. His Word establishes that man is created in the image of God and therefore is sacred and of infinite worth. Each person has the God-given right to life and respect, as each one bears the likeness of the Creator of all.

Rabbi Dr. J.H. Hertz, past Chief Rabbi of England, quotes F. Adler as saying,

> Injustice is the most flagrant manifestation of disrespect for the personality [humanity] of others.[2]

Hertz also quotes the esteemed South African General Jan C. Smuts at the inauguration of the League of Nations (predecessor of the United Nations), when he referenced Isaiah 2:1-4[3]:

> I do not know if you are aware that the League of Nations was first of all the vision of a great Jew about 3,000 years ago—the prophet Isaiah!

The value of social justice in the wider, international sphere was once very well summed up by an unidentified American jurist:

> The world owes its conception of justice to the Jewish people. God gave them to see, through the things that are ever changing, the things that never change. Compared with the meaning and majesty of this achievement, every other triumph of every other people sinks into insignificance.

The awareness of the need for a biblically based social order and just treatment of every individual within a given community has been well appreciated by Western democratic nations. However, perversion and distortion of the course of justice in many of the judicial systems today is widespread and one of the most alarming signs of their departure from God. This corruption is a somber warning and a sure indication of the danger of a nation's disintegration, as we see demonstrated in ancient cultures such as Greece and Rome.

A Pure, Whole Heart

After warning the people against the abominations of superstition and divination, Moses issues a command that sums up one's obligation to God: "*Thou shalt be wholehearted* (*tamim*) *with the* LORD *your God!*" (18:13).

The great medieval Torah commentator, Rashi (France, 1049-1105), amplifies:

> Walk with Him wholeheartedly and hope in Him. Pry not into the veiled future, but accept whatever lot befalls you. Then you will be His people and His portion.

Even as all the offerings made to the Lord at the Temple needed to be *tamim* (whole/pure) and not blemished in any way, so should our *whole* hearts be offered up to Him. When we surrender every fiber of our being to Him, and demonstrate our love for Him in wholehearted, faithful obedience, then in perfect faith and trust we confidently can leave our future entirely in His hands.

May we be among those who: *walk blamelessly (tamim) and do what is right (tzedek) and speak truth (emet) from our hearts*".[4]

Then we will constantly dwell with Him in the place of His holiness and peace, no matter the "tribulations of the world" that surround us.[5]

Suffering and Joy

This fourth "Haftarah of Consolation" presents the stark contrast between suffering and joy. The people have drained the cup of the Lord's fury (Isaiah 51:17), after forsaking the Maker of heaven and earth—the Lord their Maker (51:13). Their oppressors have afflicted them with desolation, destruction, famine and sword, and made them bow down that they might ride over them in pride.

Throughout history, the oppressors of Israel have demanded the surrender of their souls. But no matter how bleak and desperate their condition, the Jewish people do not relinquish their faith nor the spark of Divine hope in their souls. In their desolation, but with no one to take them by the hand to guide and console them, the Lord Himself says: "*I, even I, am He that comforts you*" (51:12). They are covered by the shadow of His hand.

He then proclaims to Zion: "*Thou art My people!*" (51:16). In this assurance, they can stand strong; they can shake off the dust and loose the bonds of oppression. His people have been *taken away for naught … and His Name continually blasphemed* (52:5). But God promises a new day: *My people shall know My Name; therefore, they shall know that it is I who speak: "Behold, Here am I"* (52:6).

What joyful song will break forth when all shall see, eye to eye, the Lord returning to Zion. In that day, we will greatly rejoice together with grateful hearts knowing that for all time: *The* L*ORD* *has comforted His people, He has redeemed Jerusalem* (52:9).

It is indeed a privilege, even as we endure the pain of her suffering together with her, to participate in the Lord's rebuilding and redemption of His Land, Israel and His Holy City, Jerusalem. Yeshua is preparing His throne in Zion, and with sure faith and unwavering hope in our hearts, we can look forward to the soon approaching day when the great *shofar* will sound and a cry will ring out: "Behold! Here am I!" Then, with great jubilation:

> *All the ends of the earth shall see the salvation of our God* (52:10).

---

[1] Matthew 23:23

[2] Rabbi Dr. J.I. Hertz, *Pentateuch and Haftarah*, 821.

[3] Ibid, 821.

[4] Psalm 15:1-2

[5] John 16:33

Ki Tetze - כי תצא

When You Go Out

Deuteronomy 21:10 25:19; Isaiah 54:1–10;
Galatians 3:21–47

The *parasha* begins: *When you go out (ki tetze) to war (milchamah) against your enemies … the* Lord *your God will deliver him into your hand*" (21:10).

The title is repeated later in the portion: *When you go out (ki tetze) against your enemies and are in camp (machaneh), then you shall guard yourself from every evil thing*" (23:9).

The word "war" (*milchamah)* is replaced with "camp" *(machaneh).* This places the emphasis not on the action against one's enemy but on the importance of being in a secure place when at rest. One's "camp" should not be scattered and vulnerable, but ordered and protected.

The injunction to guard against "every evil thing" implies that the real enemy is that which opposes good, that which is set to attack and destroy the spiritual values and the norms of the Kingdom of God. The greatest danger posed by the enemy of our souls, *haSatan* (the Adversary), is not physical annihilation but spiritual and moral destruction. When we are in alien territory—e.g. the unredeemed secular world—his attacks often are subtle and deceptive. The lures of sin can infiltrate through breaches we have allowed in the protective fence around our 'camp' due to neglect and failure to be on guard.

We are reminded at the outset, however, that: *The LORD your God will deliver the enemy into your hand.* We will gain the victory with His help, but we need to be aware, and stand strong and united, constantly on guard against every subtle force of evil.

The Paradox of Faith and Action

The Word of the Lord clearly expresses that our every deed and action is important in His eyes. We are constantly faced, on often a daily basis, with situations that require our response and action. The *parasha* is replete with details outlining how to deal with customary situations that arise in connection with family relationships, strangers, and even mother birds.

The reference to mother birds, in 22:6-7, underscores the significance of sensitivity and compassion towards animals. Although this is called the "least" commandment by the Sages, it is understood that the underlying principle also should be reflected in our dealings with fellow humans. In fact it is an important element of the "greatest" commandment of loving one another.

Yeshua taught His disciples that faith in God should empower their actions.

> *Have faith in God. Truly, I say to you, whoever says to this mountain, "Be taken up and cast into the sea," and does not doubt in his heart, but believes that what he says will come to pass, it will be done for him.*[1]

The esteemed leader of the first congregation of Yeshua's followers in Jerusalem stressed:

> *...Faith by itself, if it has no works, is dead. But one may say, "You have faith and I have works; show me your faith apart from your works, and I by my works will show you my faith."*[2]

This indicates that faith is not an intellectual exercise—a matter of doctrinal beliefs. As Rabbi Tzvi Freeman well describes: "Intellect can orbit about the truth forever, but it doesn't have feet to land."[3] Faith gives feet to our belief! Faith enables us to stand on the Truth. In this, faith resembles love. It is only given life, integrity and vitality when it is reflected in outward action.

Faith is not blind. It is an inner vision and knowledge of the One in whom we believe. Once our hearts are yielded to God we understand that our faithful actions are important. At the same time, we need to have unwavering certainty that only His perfect will determines the outcome of any endeavor. Our health, our material gain, our very lives are in His hands. He is ultimately our Protector and Provider.

Nevertheless, as a father does his grown children, our Father gives us the responsibility to make decisions on how to conduct our lives on a daily basis. The choice is ours to study and grow in wisdom, understanding and application of His Word, to eat nourishing food, to work conscientiously for our living, to care for others, and to not take unnecessary risks with our lives. We must walk in faith … but diligently act. This is the paradox and the challenge!

The Month of Elul

The month of *Elul* is the sixth month of the Hebrew calendar. It leads up to *Rosh HaShanah* (New Year) which falls on the first day of the seventh month of *Tishrei*.[4] Why is this biblical New Year significant and of interest to believers in Yeshua?

In Jewish tradition the purpose of *Rosh HaShanah* (also called the Day of Remembrance) in the Festival Cycle is to acknowledge that the world is governed only by God's will. He is Creator and Sovereign over all of nature and humanity. This may seem elementary at first glance, but in fact the implications are vast and deep.

A full month is devoted to implanting this powerful principle in our hearts. Every day during *Elul,* Psalm 27 is recited and the *shofar* (ram's horn) is blown[5]. The alternating plaintive cries and victorious blasts of the *shofar* are fitting sounds to stir our souls to awareness and repentance. We are re-awakened to the glory and majesty of the King of the Universe, and can reaffirm the *shalom* of the Prince of Peace reigning in our hearts.

These solemn assemblies are observed "in camp"—in community. But it is important to note that the days of *Elul* also focus in a specific way on the individual. They prepare one for the impending appointed times of the Days of Awe": *Rosh HaShanah* followed ten days later by *Yom Kippur* (The Day of Atonement). The stirring day when the account of our deeds of the preceding year is brought before the Throne of God and a ruling is accordingly passed that affects the year ahead. The basic principle in consideration here is, "You shall reap what you sow."

As we honor the universal sovereignty of our Creator, we are reminded that on the day that Yeshua returns in glory to Jerusalem as the King of kings, He will be the Judge of each and of all. Every nation (Isaiah 2:4) and each individual (Romans 14:12) will stand before His throne of judgment. We will be held accountable for our deeds. What did we do with the gift of life and the talents we were given by our Father?

Inventory Time!

Every responsible citizen submits his or her tax return. And every business knows the positive need for—and also the effort involved in—an annual inventory assessment. Similarly, the month of *Elul* is a time we are encouraged to take a serious inventory of our lives. It is an opportunity to review the past year and take note of the health and growth of one's character and relationships, and of one's dealings with others. Have I grown positively, in loving-kindness and in truth? Have my actions been in line with God's Word? Is my life reflecting more of the light of our Messiah and Lord, Yeshua?

Wherever we can answer in the affirmative, we rejoice. And when we notice some "breaches in the fence," we can repair them in sincere repentance and begin to reinforce the weak areas "*B'ezrat HaShem*," with the Lord's help.

The tone and essence of *Elul*, with *Rosh HaShanah* and *Yom Kippur* following, is not that of dismal foreboding but of celebration and gratitude. Indeed, the name *Elul (aleph, lamed, vav, lamed)* can be read as a Hebrew acronym:

> *Ani le'dodi ve'dodi li—I am my Beloved's and my Beloved is mine* (Song of Songs 2:16).

This is our inspiration and motivation. We can rejoice in the gracious favor of our Beloved, and rest in the knowledge that our lives are in His hands. We can indeed 'camp' securely, knowing that by the power of His Holy Spirit we have been given victory over our enemies, both physical and spiritual.

May we live our lives every day, every month, and every year, to the honor of His Name and to the glory of our Father in heaven.

---

1 Mark 11:22-23

2 James 2:17-18

3 Rabbi Tzvi Freeman, *Supermind*, Daily Dose, Chabad.org, 1 August, 2008.

4 Leviticus 23:24

5 Numbers 29:1

Ki Tavo - כי תבוא

When You Come

Deuteronomy 26:1–29:8; Isaiah 60:1–22;
Romans 11:1–15

The introductory verse of this week's *parasha* was recited as one of the blessings in the Temple in Jerusalem when offerings were made of the annual tithes and firstfruits of the harvest (*bikkurim*). These offerings were an expression of gratitude for the land the people had inherited and for the material benefits they derived from it.

The verse demonstrates clearly that it was God's will and by His power that the people of Israel were established in the land:

> *When you come to the Land that the* Lord *your God is giving you as an inheritance…* (26:1).

The Triple Covenant - People, Scriptures, Land

The Torah describes three covenants established by God with Israel.

- **Holy People.**

  The first covenant is cut with Abraham, and is referred to as "*the covenant between the pieces*" (Genesis 15:1-21). God guarantees Abraham progeny and boundaries. He will be the father of countless children and through him *"all the nations will be blessed."*

The Abrahamic covenant establishes the reality of an elect people of God; a people chosen to enter into a personal, intimate relationship with Him; an extended family that can 'know' God and call Him "our God".

The outward sign of this covenant is circumcision, the essence of which is circumcision of the heart (Genesis 17:4-13).

- **Holy Scriptures.**

The second covenant is established at Sinai. Abraham's family is now ready to receive more concretely the Almighty's guidance and instructions for life. God takes His place as King and reveals the laws of His Kingdom, intended for the blessing and prosperity of His people (Exodus 34:27-29).

The external sign of this covenant is *Shabbat* (the Sabbath). The spirit of Shabbat is peace and wholeness.

The Torah revealed at Sinai can be considered as the *ketubah* or marriage document and pledge given by God to Israel. Shabbat is the 'wedding ring' of the union—the visible symbol of God's eternal love and commitment to His people, and their covenant faithfulness to Him (Exodus 31:16-17). God's Word is incarnated, and given living expression in the *Brit Chadasha*, the Renewed Covenant, in *Adon ha'Shabbat* (the Lord of the Sabbath) Yeshua.

- **Holy Land.**

The third covenant is described in this week's *parasha.* It is established upon Israel's entry into the land God is giving them as an inheritance. It is a covenant of *arevut* (mutual responsibility) between the people and God, as well as each individual towards the other. Once the people are settled in the Land, a central feature of this covenant is the ceremony of "first-fruits"—offerings of thankfulness to the Lord for the land and its produce. Another feature is giving of tithes to the Levites and to the poor (26:1-15)—an illustration that gratitude and responsible giving go hand in hand.

The symbol of the third covenant is a natural stone altar, as opposed to an altar of man-made material[1]. This is the first structure the Israelites are commanded to set up once they cross over and take possession of the Promised Land[2]. The altar is the place of sacrificial and yet joyful offering.

This speaks to us of the free-willed offering of our lives in obedience to the One who first laid down His life for us. In the power of the Holy Spirit and in union with the Father, Yeshua demonstrated that willing sacrifice leads to joy unspeakable.

Serve with Joyful Hearts

The offering of *Bikkurim*, First Fruits, is brought at the start of the Festival of *Shavu'ot* (Feast of Weeks - Pentecost)[3]. The people of Israel come up to Jerusalem from all directions, bringing the fruits of their harvest as gifts unto the Lord. They come in colorful procession, bedecked with flowers and responding with music, singing and dancing. It is a joyous time as thousands of pilgrims fill the holy city and celebrate the goodness of God and His bounteous provision.

In the same way, we are exhorted to appreciate all the Lord provides and to give in return with cheerful hearts. Everything we have is a gift from our faithful Father, who delights in giving with a free and open hand to His children and to all His creatures.

We need to take note of the reason given for the awful curses listed toward the conclusion of the *parasha*:

> *... the fact that you did not serve the* Lord *your God with joy and gladness of heart when you had plenty of everything!* (28:47).

This presents us with a challenge today. Do we rejoice in the fact that we are children of God, and that we can enjoy the fullness of that relationship in our Lord and Redeemer, Yeshua? Are our hearts lifted up in gratitude every day for the life He has given us and the good things we enjoy? Do we celebrate the "good way" He has set down in Scripture, and walk in that way with joy?

Repent and Rejoice

Every new day is filled with innumerable signs of God's love. The beauty of the sky, the dawn, the sunset ... all of nature is filled with His glory. Every move we make, the smallest aspect of the daily pattern of our lives, literally every breath we take is infused with His grace and presence. When we allow ourselves to approach these moments with a sense of wonder, common-place occurrences can become transcendent and filled with holiness.

To our amazement we realize that not only are these indications of His love for us, they are symbols of His desire to be loved by us in return. Each moment therefore carries the opportunity to respond in love to the Beloved of our souls.

During the month of *Elul* we have an opportunity specifically to examine our hearts and to trust the Holy Spirit to lead us in recognizing areas of weakness or sin in the past year. Now is the time to take responsibility for our actions and repent—

to turn our hearts and guide our steps back to the way of God and to put things right where we can.

May we repent of any ingratitude or envy or of harboring feelings that we "deserve more"—in other words, of anything that shows that we have set our *selves* at the center of our lives, in the Lord's place. Our highest joy is to be found in Him alone. With God at the center we can rejoice together with free hearts, filled with joy and peace as we enter the gates of the New Year in anticipation of another *Shanah Tovah*—a "good year" in His Presence.

Let us come into His presence with thanksgiving; let us make a joyful noise to Him with songs of praise! [4]

---

[1] Isaiah 65:3

[2] Exodus 27:1-8

[3] Numbers 28:26

[4] Psalm 95:2

Nitzavim - נִצָּבִים

You Are Standing

Deuteronomy 29:9–30:20; Isaiah 61:10–63:9;
Colossians 3:12–17

The three consecutive portions of *Ki Tetze*, *Ki Tavo* and *Nitzavim* are interconnected: *"When You Go Out," "When You Come," and "You Are Standing."* Their names describe the actions of going, coming, and standing.

The context of *Ki Tetze* is going out to war. We can apply this on a personal level. In the yet unredeemed and often hostile world in which we live, we can find ourselves camped in enemy territory and often involved in a battle. Our trust and hope must be firmly anchored in the faithful protection and guidance of the Almighty, the Lord of Hosts.

We also are enjoined to actively and wisely "guard against evil"—to actively protect our hearts and our homes from the onslaught of the enemy forces in all their blatant and subtle forms. The desire of those who love the Father of all is for one's home to be a *mikdash me'at*, a miniature temple designed to house and honor Him; a sanctuary where the soul finds peace and rest. A further extension is that our bodies are living temples in Messiah, housing the Holy Spirit in our hearts:

> *Do you not know that your body is a temple of the Holy Spirit within you, which you have from God? You are not your own; you were bought with a price. So glorify God in your body.*[1]

Ki Tavo, "When You Come," is set in the context of coming up joyfully to the place of the Lord's choosing to bring offerings, to come before Him with grateful praise and to celebrate together in His Presence. Thus we see that on the one hand we are carefully and diligently to be on guard, protecting all the precious gifts given to us by our loving, heavenly Father. On the other hand, there are times to come together before Him in joyful abandonment and grateful assurance of His provision and protection.

This week's portion, *Nitzavim*, emphasizes that at all times we are given the pronouncement *to stand!* We are constantly to be aware of the One before whom we stand. In so doing we can stand our ground against the enemy, secure in our Messiah and Lord who is our strong tower and refuge in times of trouble; and our everlasting peace. When at last we come before His throne of judgment, we know we can stand in confidence and delight—even as we are reminded in this week's *haftarah* (the last of the seven Sabbaths of Consolation):

> *For He has clothed me with garments of salvation and arrayed me with a robe of righteousness, as a bridegroom bedecked with a garland, and as a bride adorned with jewels.*[2]

The Covenant of "One"

In the opening verses of *Nitzavim*, God gathers His people together at the border of the Promised Land:

> *... so that you [all] may pass over [as one] into the Covenant of God that He is making with you today* (29:12).

The marriage covenant unites bride and groom as "one"—a unified whole—renouncing all others. In God's covenant with His people, they pass over from their previous status and renounce all other spiritual attachments in order to enter this exclusive relationship of intimacy with their Redeemer.

Perhaps it is the primacy of this covenant relationship that Yeshua alludes to in a seemingly shocking declaration in Luke 8:21. While teaching a large crowd, someone informs Him that His mother and brothers are waiting outside to see Him and He replies:

> *"My mother and brothers are those who hear God's Word and put it into practice."*

Luke records another occasion when a woman calls out from the crowd,

> *"Blessed is the mother who gave you birth and nursed you!"*

Yeshua counters:

> *"Blessed, rather, are those who hear the Word of God and obey it!"* (11:27-28).

His mother *Miryam* (Mary) wholeheartedly did just that, and was indeed blessed in her faithfulness.

Yeshua constantly emphasizes the need to seek first the Kingdom of God—His Kingship in our lives—then all other good things will follow. If we first love Him and are in right, exclusive, covenant relationship with our Father God, then the honor and love we extend to our parents, our siblings, our spouse, and our children will be in right order. Consequently, we will enjoy the blessed harmony and delight of *echad* (oneness) that God exemplifies in His Oneness and in His covenant of love.

We enter this unity by His Spirit of holiness. Paul alludes to this precious privilege in 1 Corinthians 6:17,

> *... he who is united to the Lord becomes one spirit with Him.*

This is also the passion behind Yeshua's final powerful prayer to the Father on behalf of all those who would believe in Him:

> *"...that they may all be one; even as Thou, Father, art in me, and I in Thee, that they also may be in us, so that the world may believe that Thou hast sent me. The glory which Thou hast given me I have given to them, that they may be one even as we are one, I in them and Thou in me, that they may become perfectly one, so that the world may know that Thou hast sent me and hast loved them even as Thou hast loved me."*[3]

A Kingdom People

The Word makes clear that in the Kingdom of God we enter into more than an individual and personal relationship with God. We also enter into covenant relationship with a people. The opening verses of our *parasha* state: *You [plural] are all standing ... so that you may pass over as one (*29:10-11*)* into the covenant of God. Covenant unites and binds us together. Many individuals become one people, one kingdom, one holy priesthood.

An interesting declaration is made in verse 14:

> *"[God's covenant is made] with him who is standing here today and with him who is not with us today."*

This indicates that the covenant at Sinai is established for all future generations of the people Israel. It also points to the radical extension of the Kingdom of God, in the person of His Son Yeshua, to include all those He would call from the nations to be grafted in to the family tree of Israel[4].

Ruth is a beautiful illustration and precursor of this; she left her foreign gods and chose to join herself to the God of Israel and His people. She proclaimed to Naomi, *"...your people shall be my people, and your God my God"*.[5] And through her faith and faithfulness, the kingly line of David was established and Messiah was born!

In his letter to the believers in Rome, Paul highlights the mission of Yeshua's life on earth: He came as a suffering servant to Israel, those already in the covenant of Abraham, Isaac and Jacob,

> *...to show God's truthfulness, in order to confirm the promises given to the patriarchs, and in order that the Gentiles might glorify God for His mercy. As it is written, "Therefore I will praise thee among the Gentiles, and sing to thy name"; and again it is said, "Rejoice, O Gentiles, with His people".*[6]

In the Almighty's great mercy and love, a way was made from before the beginning of time, through the atoning death and glorious resurrection of Yeshua, for all peoples to enter into the eternal covenant. All may cross over the chasm of sin and godlessness and be joined in relationship with our Father God and united with His chosen people and enter His royal priesthood.

Being Built Up

God established Yeshua as King and entrusted the Kingdom and its people to Him.[7] In Him the Kingdom of God burst forth into all the earth and is advancing and being built together until that glorious day when the King appears in His majesty to take up His throne in Jerusalem.

Until then, we are mutually responsible to love one another and to build up one another as one people. United in Messiah, we can stand together at the Mount of revelation, Sinai, while awaiting the fulfillment of the Son of Man's climactic consummation at Mount Zion.

Even as God is one, His eternal covenant is one, established from time immemorial with one people, who are in relationship with one King, building one Kingdom. The *ketubah*—written agreement for a covenant relationship—is God's eternal and unchanging Word first given at Sinai. That same

Word subsequently became incarnate in Yeshua, the one who is the judge and righteous King.[8]

Therefore, in agreement with the prophet Isaiah in the *haftarah*, let us say:

> *For the sake of Zion I will not keep silent, and for Jerusalem's sake I will not rest, until her vindication goes forth as brightness, and her salvation as a burning torch* (62:1).

> *Say to the daughter of Zion, "Behold your salvation has come!"* (62:11).

And the Bridegroom says: "*I will rejoice in Jerusalem, and be glad in My people*" (65:19).

---

1 I Corinthians 6:19-20

2 Isaiah 61:10-11

3 John 17:21-23

4 Romans 11:17

5 Ruth 1:16

6 Romans 15:8-10

7 Revelation 11:15

8 Isaiah 32:1; 33:22

Va'yelekh - וילך
And Moses Went

Deuteronomy 31:1–30; Isaiah 61:10–63:9;
Hebrews 13:1–8

The remainder of the book of *Devarim* describes the last days of Moses, including his final address to the children of Israel. Part of his farewell will be rendered as a beautiful Song, in the following portion *Ha'azinu*, which is reminiscent of his Song at the Sea after the Lord's deliverance of His people from Egyptian slavery. Then the Torah will conclude with Moses extending his blessing upon all the people of Israel, recorded in the last *parasha* of the book, *Ve'zot ha'Brakha* - "And this is the Blessing."

O God our Help!

Psalm 90 is accredited to Moses: *The Prayer of Moses, the man of God.*

Rabbi Hertz attests that Moses might well have written this psalm at this latter time of his life.[1] It is a meditation upon the fleeting life of man in contrast to the durability of the rugged wilderness mountains through which the Israelites had wandered for forty years. But even the towering mountains shrink and seem transitory before the greatness and grandeur of the One who created them and existed in eternity before they were set in place.

Hertz records the splendid hymn penned by Watts, based on Moses' psalm[2]:

> O God our help in ages past, our hope for years to come,
> Our shelter from the stormy blast, and our eternal home.
> Before the hills in order stood, or earth received her frame,
> From everlasting Thou art God, to endless years the same.
> A thousand ages in Thy sight, are like an evening gone,
> Short as the watch that ends the night, before the rising sun.

When Moses is a hundred and twenty years old he says,

> "*I can no more go out and come in*" (31:2).

Although we are told that when he died his vision was clear and his natural strength unabated, Moses no longer could "*go out*" to war, nor "*come in*" to the Promised Land with the Israelites. He no longer could accompany them on their journey—but he blesses and encourages the people with these powerful words:

> "*Be strong and of good courage, fear not, nor be in dread of them, for the LORD your God, He it is that goes with you. He will not fail you, nor forsake you*" (31:6).

The Witness of the Word and the Song

Moses delivers the written Torah to the Levitical priests and the elders of Israel, along with his inspired teaching and commentary. He then commands that every seven years, at the Feast of Tabernacles in Jerusalem, they are to assemble all the people—men, women and children, and the stranger within their gates—and publicly read the Torah before the whole assembly (31:10-12).

This is to be done in order that:

> ... *they may hear, and that they may learn to fear the LORD your God, and observe to do all the words of this law [Torah]* (31:12).

This practice guarantees that every seven-year-old child will hear the words and teachings of the Lord, and that they will be reiterated to the entire nation every seven years.

Moses and Joshua are summoned by the Lord to the tent of meeting, where He *appeared in the Tent in a pillar of cloud* (31:15). Sadly, He tells Moses that, in spite of all they have seen and heard, the Israelites will rebel against His Word and go astray after foreign gods. They will forsake the God of Israel. His face will then be hidden from them, and they will be beset by many evils and troubles.

The Lord exhorts Moses to write his farewell song and teach it to the children of Israel. It will be a testimony to the everlasting Presence and goodness of God. It also will be a constant witness of Israel's separation from Him, but will remind them of the opportunity to repent of their ways and return their God.

L'Shanah Tovah! - To a Good Year!

The Psalmist declares:

> *Ashrei ha'am yod'ei teruah ...!*
>
> *Blessed are the people who know the joyful sound [of the shofar].*[3]

The Jewish New Year, *Rosh HaShanah,* is associated with the blowing *(teruah)* of the shofar. There are three basic notes sounded on the ram's horn, which elicit a variety of meanings and responses. They all accord with the focus of the season, which is *teshuvah* (repentance) or turning from one's own stubborn and selfish path and returning to the true ways of the Father.

- The first is *tekiah,* a long, straight note. The clear, unbroken cry sounds like an alarm or wake-up call: "Stop and examine your life, for it is of limited duration. Get your priorities in line with your Father's will for your life!"

- The second note consists of three broken blasts, called *shevarim*. These remind us of the 'brokenness' of mankind—broken and bent out of shape by sin.
- These are followed by nine short, staccato blasts called *teruah*, which echo the sobbing of a truly repentant heart, crying to the Father with a longing to return to the true, pure state for which it was created.

The concluding sound is a final *tekiah*—but the note is held steady and extended for as long as the person has air! It is a dramatic blast, increasing in intensity, and brings the hearer as it were to "tip-toes" in expectancy. It seems to echo and become part of one long, eternal sound of God's unity—the perfect delight and harmony of God's one-ness that draws together all who have ears to hear and to "know" it.

What comfort it brings and what glorious hope it stirs in our souls—that, in truth, the sound of the Great Shofar of Redemption and Salvation is never stilled. It grows louder and louder, until the final, awesome Day of the Lord. That great Day of Jubilee will dawn when the King of the Universe suddenly appears and judges the nations, with His throne established on the holy hill of Zion.

He will reign and His Kingdom will endure forever and ever. There will then be no need for the broken, sobbing sounds of the shofar. They will be stilled eternally by shouts of joy and the unbroken fullness of the Lord's Presence.

---

[1] Rabbi Dr. J.I. Hertz, The *Pentateuch and Haftorahs*, 887.

[2] Ibid, 887

[3] Psalm 89:15

Ha'azinu - האזינו

Give Ear

Deuteronomy 32:1–52; 2 Samuel 22:1–51;
Revelation 15:1–4

As instructed by the Lord, Moses delivers this song to the Israelites on the last day of his life. An inspired poem of stirring beauty, his prophetic words describe the future destiny of God's people. It reflects the truth that all history is the revelation and expression of God's creative love and care which are constantly at work by His Spirit towards and through His people.

The song opens with the appointment of heaven and earth as witnesses and guarantors of God's everlasting covenant with Israel.

> *Give ear (ha'azinu), O heavens, and I will speak; and let the earth hear (ti'shma) the words of my mouth* (32:1)

The Hebrew word *ha'azin* (to incline one's ear–*oh'zen*) connotes a greater awareness and acceptance of the spoken word than the more commonly used term *sh'ma*, to hear.

By using the word *ha'azin* in connection with heaven, and the word *sh'ma* with earth, Moses is indicating that the covenant and its implementation is initiated by God from heaven and those on earth function in a secondary capacity in its consummation.

Whatever takes place on earth according to God's will begins with action initiated in heaven. This concept underscores the importance of prayer as a powerful means of participating in the active momentum of the "heavenly realm" and its outworking on the earth. We open our ears to God's Word given from heaven, and He inclines His ear to our prayers offered in response.

Rain and Dew

My teaching shall drop as the rain; My speech shall distil as the dew; As rainstorms on the grass and showers on the herb (32:2).

Moses uses the striking metaphor of precipitation—different forms of rain and the dew— to effectively draw attention to the varying aspects of God's Word. The teachings of Torah sometimes fall lightly but persistently like a gentle rain, softening and preparing the soil. Even the hardness of stubborn wills and stony hearts, and the inflexibility of stiff necks, can be softened by the water of the Word and prepared to receive seed and life.

The loving promises of God alight gently like the dew, refreshing and sustaining the soul, even through dry seasons. Herbs, more delicate than large, sturdier plants, require steady watering, light and sustaining showers to encourage and sustain growth. We can compare this to the regular study of the Word necessary to feed and permeate our souls as we grow spiritually. The heavier rainstorms descend on fields of grass, that which is rooted and established and strong. These can be compared to the "latter rain" outpourings of the Spirit that cleanse, soak, and ultimately cause the bringing forth of much fruit in the life of a righteous, devoted student of the Word.

Just as the Almighty controls the wind and the rain, He continually is at work in the unfolding history of His elect nation, Israel, and in the lives of all His children throughout the earth. His ultimate purpose—ever drawing closer—is the full redemption of Israel and the nations through His Son, the Messiah, who was appointed for the task before the foundation of the world.

> *He was destined before the foundation of the world but was made manifest at the end of the times for your sake. Through him you have confidence in God, who raised him from the dead and gave him glory, so that your faith and hope are in God.*[1]

Our God, the Rock

> *Ascribe greatness to our God, the Rock, His work is perfect and all His ways are just. A God of faithfulness and no injustice, righteous and upright is He* (32:3b-4).

This glorious outburst of praise declares the true character of the God of Israel. Who could not worship Him? Every word He speaks and every decree He issues is perfect.

At the heart of our faith and trust in Him is the belief that, in His infinite wisdom and perfectly righteous character, our Father knows and does what is best for His children. Often in the face of natural disaster and the inexplicable tragedy of man's inhumanity to man, we are tempted to cry out, "Why, Lord?" But even when all else fails we can trust our fully righteous and compassionate God to lift us up and enable us to stand on the Rock that is immovable and cannot be shaken.

One observer creatively describes that during our brief journey through time we see only a limited view of the tapestry the Lord is weaving; and what we see is only the disordered underside. On the day Messiah returns in glory as King of the whole earth, all will be revealed in its beauty and glowing perfection. The tapestry will be seen to be a masterly work of art. Till then we can persevere in the certain knowledge of

His everlasting love and support, and we can joyfully proclaim as does King David:

> *The* L*ORD lives; blessed be my Rock.*[2]

Yeshurun Forsakes God

The name *Yeshurun* is applied to Israel in terms of its ideal calling as the people of God: to be *yashar*—moral, straight and upright—and to shine the light of God's justice and truth in the world. Sadly, however, we read in this week's *parasha*:

> *Then Yeshurun became fat and kicked … And he forsook God, who had made him; And regarded as worthless the Rock of his salvation* (32:15).

Once the people settled in the Land they became "fat" and prosperous, which proved to be the downfall of their moral, spiritual, and upright selves. They became spiritually bent and weak, and forsook their Maker and the righteous ways of His Word.

Israel turned aside to other foreign powers and alien gods that could do nothing for them but instead led them into ruin and frustration. In their defection from the light of the Kingdom of God they descended inevitably into the hostile, pessimistic, and futile domains of darkness.

The primary purpose of the Song of Moses is to confront the children of Israel with the truth that when they find themselves immersed in the suffering that results from their rebellion against God, He nonetheless remains the firm, unchanging Rock of their Salvation (*Yeshuah*). If they will turn to Him in repentance, and acknowledge that He is the only true Source of life and redemption, He will be there to lift them up and to straighten their bentness so that once again they may be called *Yeshurun!*

Shabbat Shuva - Sabbath of Repentance

The Shabbat on which *Ha'azinu* is read in synagogues often falls during the ten Days of Awe between *Rosh HaShanah* and *Yom Kippur*, and is called the Sabbath of Repentance. *Shuva* (return) is the root word of *teshuvah* (repentance).

On such occasions, the regular *haftarah*, 2 Samuel 22:1-51, is not read but is replaced by three related passages from the minor prophets: Hosea 14:2-10; Micah 7:18-20; and Joel 2:15-27.

- The prophet Hosea's message is a heartfelt reminder of God's unfailing love for Israel. He exhorts them:

  Return, O Israel, unto the LORD your God; for you have stumbled in your iniquity. Take with you words, and return to the LORD (14:2-3a).

  Hosea points out that God does not want animal sacrifices, but longs to hear words of confession and repentance offered from sincere hearts.

  When they turn from the idolatry of the work of their hands, the Lord promises to heal and restore the children of Israel. Then they will flourish in His love, and their Land will be healed. Once again it will produce grain and *blossom as the vine* (14:8). And Israel will become convinced that:

  ... the ways of the Lord are right, and the righteous do walk in them... (14:9).

- The prophet Micah echoes this promise of the faithful God:

  ... [who] delights in mercy and will again have compassion and *will cast all their sins into the depths of the sea* (7:18-19).

- The prophet Joel stresses the connection between the restored relationship of the people to their God and the consequent blessing on the Land. When they repent and return to Him, then:

  The threshing floors shall be filled with grain, and the vats shall overflow with wine and oil (2:24).

  Then the people will praise the Name of the Lord their God and never again be ashamed.

And you shall know that I am in the midst of Israel, and that I am the LORD your God, and there is none else! (2:27a).

[1] 1 Peter 1:20-21

[2] 2 Samuel 22:47

Ve'zot ha'Brakha - וזאת הברכה

And this is the Blessing

Deuteronomy 33:1–34:12; Joshua 1:1–18;
Matthew 17:1–9

> *And this is the blessing with which Moses, the man of God, blessed the sons of Israel before his death* (33:1).

Moses is about to set out on his final ascent. He goes alone to meet with his God, just as he did on Mount Sinai. He passes through the camp as a father taking leave of his children, and he blesses the various tribes. Finally, he raises his hands over the whole multitude for his last general blessing, which is one of great beauty, encouragement, and comfort. It has remained a source of reassurance and blessing for all God's children through the ages:

> *There is none like unto God, O Yeshurun, Who rides upon the heaven as thy help … The eternal God is a dwelling place, and underneath are the everlasting arms…* (33:26-27).

A Fiery Law

At the start of the *parasha* we find an intriguing phrase:

> *At His right hand was a fiery law [esh-daht] unto them* (33:2).

Esh-daht can be read as "fire-become-law". God's Law or Torah was majestically presented at Sinai to Moshe and the people through holy fire. The Bible records that the Torah was written by the "finger" or Spirit of God. Traditional Jewish writings suggest that it was written in letters of black fire on a parchment of white fire, and that seventy tongues of flame came forth at Mt. Sinai, representing the seventy nations of the world—signifying that God's Word was meant for all peoples of all tongues.

This adds another dimension to our understanding of the outpouring of the Holy Spirit experienced by the followers of Yeshua who had gathered at the mount of the House of God to celebrate the festival of *Shavu'ot* (Acts 2). Jerusalem was bustling with the crowds of Jews and God-fearers, from across the Land and also from the nations, that had come up to Jerusalem to celebrate the Feast. To their amazement miraculous tongues of fire appeared, reminiscent of the first Shavuot at Mount Sinai, and came to rest upon the disciples. Consequently, their inspired speech in diverse languages enabled the gathered crowds to hear and understand their message of the Torah-Incarnate Messiah.

The same good news is applicable today. The Son went forth from God's right hand of salvation, became flesh and tabernacled amongst us; and when by faith we receive Him, the Holy Spirit writes the dynamic fire of His Torah upon our hearts.

Fire is a positive, constructive element that generates warmth, illumination, energy and movement. If uncontrolled, however, it becomes a raging, destructive force. We see the same phenomenon with *esh-daht*. Unless controlled by the truth of God's Word given at Sinai—confirmed and echoed at Mount Zion—religious zeal can become a raging, violent fire that brings death instead of life, hatred in place of holiness.

Sit at His Feet and Receive

The picture presented in 33:3 is one of peace and order as the "holy ones" sit humbly and happily at the feet of God, receiving His instruction:

> *Yea, He loved His people; all those consecrated to Him were in His hand; and they sat down at His feet; every one receiving of His words.*

This picture is perfectly replicated in the scene described in Luke 10:41-42, when Yeshua visits the home of His friends in Bethany. Martha is busily occupied with preparations, while Mary is content to sit at the Lord's feet, not wanting to lose the precious opportunity of hearing His words of wisdom. Martha becomes resentful at having to do all the work single-handedly, but Yeshua gently reprimands her:

> *"Martha, Martha, you are anxious and troubled about many things; one thing is needful. Mary has chosen the good portion, which shall not be taken from her."*

This is a gentle reminder to us too—that we not become so busy and occupied with serving the Lord that we neglect to sit quietly and humbly at His feet, listening to His teaching and receiving life-giving words of wisdom.

Moses declares, "*Yes, He loves His people.*" The words of life from God's heart of great and infinite love are for *all* people, from every tribe, nation, and tongue—all the "holy ones" who freely enter His Covenant and honor Him as King.

Simchat Torah - The Joy of the Word

This final *parasha* of the Torah is read at the conclusion of the Festival Cycle on the holiday of *Simchat Torah*. Following the week-long Feast of Tabernacles, it completes and "crowns" the Feast as well as the year-long cycle.

During the celebration of *Simchat Torah* in synagogues, Torah scrolls are removed from their Arks and, accompanied by much singing and rejoicing, they are paraded amongst the congregation. The Torah is embraced and kissed, and people joyfully dance with the scrolls as an expression of their love for the Word of God. It is a great celebration, which the children especially enjoy when candies are happily tossed to them as reminders of the sweetness of the Torah.

We can also celebrate with joy in the knowledge that the "fire of life" that Moshe passed on to Israel from God became enfleshed in Yeshua the Messiah. He fulfilled all the "just requirements" of the Torah and was obedient even unto a cursed death on a tree—that all peoples might in Him have access to eternal and abundant life in the Kingdom of God

We celebrate Yeshua's life as the Living Torah. This "word of life" planted in our hearts, our innermost beings, by the Spirit of holiness, enables us to be reconciled in right, loving relationship with our Abba Father and we are empowered to walk in His paths of righteousness.

It is written in this week's *haftarah:*

> *This book of Torah shall not leave your mouth; meditate thereon in order to observe all that is in it, for then you will be successful in all your ways and then you will prosper* (Joshua 1:8).

This is the "good portion" He offers us, and the good way walked by Yeshua Himself. As we "taste and see" that He is good, let us choose to continually sit at His feet, to learn of His Father's ways, and to steadfastly walk after Him.

Chazak, chazak, ve'nitchazek!
Be strong, be strong, and let us strengthen one another!

Appendix 1

Blessing Before the Study of Torah

Barukh Atah Adonai Melekh Ha'Olam
Asher natan lanu Torat Emet
Ve'chayai olam nata be'tocheinu
Barukh Atah Adonai, noten ha'Torah
Amen

Blessed are You, O Lord our God, King of the Universe
Who gave us the Torah of truth
And implanted eternal life within us.
Blessed are You, O Lord, Giver of the Torah.
Amen

Almighty God, King of heaven and earth, open our eyes that we may see wonderful things in Your Torah.
(Psalm 119:18)

Blessing After the Study of Torah

Father, we thank you for the precious gift of Your Word.

Its ways are ways of pleasantness and all its paths are peace.
It is a tree of life for those who take hold of it…
(Proverbs 3:17-18)

As we take hold of the tree of life we trust, by Your grace, that our lives may shine forth the glory of our Savior Yeshua and bring the light of Your Presence and Truth to this dark and needy world.

For the sake of Your Name.
Amen

Appendix II

Hebrew Pronunciation Guide

Vowels – Transliteration and pronunciation

a – *ah* as in 'father'	As in the letter *aleph / ah'lef*; Abba (Father) / *Ah'bah*
ai – *ai* as in 'Thai'	*Dai!* (Enough!); *El Shaddai* (God our Provider)
e – *eh* as in 'bed'	As in the letter *bet* (*beht*)
ei – *ei* as in 'eight'	As in the letter *reish*, B'reishit (Genesis) / *B'rei'sheet*
i – *ee* as in 'beet'	As in the letter *gimel / gee'mel*; *ani* (I or me) / *ah'nee*
o – *oh* as in 'home'	As in *yom* (day) and *Shalom*.
u – oo as in 'noon'	As in the letter *nun / noon*

Hebrew letters—name, transliteration and numerical value

Transliterated consonants are pronounced as in English. Exceptions are marked with an asterisk.

1 א / aleph / *ah'lef*

2 בּ / bet / *beht* used at the beginning of a word

ב / vet / *veht* used within a word

3 ג / gimel / *gee'mehl*

4 ד / dalet / *dah'leht*

5 ה / heh / *hei*

6 ו / vav / *vahv*

7 ז / zayin / *zai'yeen*

8 ח / chet / *chet* – **ch* is a light fricative sound as in the Scottish 'loch'

9 ט / tet / *teht*

10 י / yod / *yood*

20 כּ / kaf / *kahf* – when used at the beginning of a word

כ / khaf / *khaf* – when used within a word

– * *kh* is a guttural sound as in 'Bach'

ך / khaf sofit / *khaf soh'feet* – when used as the final letter of a word

30 ל / lamed / *lah'mehd*

40 מ / mem / *mehm*

ם / mem sofit / *mem soh'feet* – when used as the final letter of a word

50 נ / nun / *noon*

ן / nun sofit / *nun soh'feet* – when used as the final letter of a word

60 ס / samech / *sah'mech*

70 ע / ayin / *ah'yeen*

80 פּ / peh / *pei* – when used at the beginning of a word

פ / feh / *fei* – when used within a word

ף / feh sofit / fei *soh'feet* – when used as the final letter of a word

90 צ / tzadi / *tzah'dee* - **tz* is a sound similar to the zz in 'pizza'

ץ / tzadi sofit / *tzadi soh'feet* – when used as the final letter of a word

100 ק / kuf / *koof*

200 ר / reish / *reish*

300 שׁ / shin / *sheen* – indicated by a dot on the right hand branch of the letter

שׂ / sin / *seen* – indicated by a dot on the left hand branch of the letter

400 ת / tav / *tahv*

Bibliography

Ariel, Rabbi Yisrael, *The Odyssey of the Third Temple*, G. Israel Publications and Productions Ltd., Jerusalem, Israel.

Artson, Rabbi Bradley Shavit, *The Bedside Torah*, Contemporary Books, USA.

Cook, Roy J., comp., *101 Famous Poems, An Anthology*. Contemporary Books, USA, 1958.

Etz Hayim, Torah and Commentary, The Jewish Publication Society, The Rabbinical Assembly of Conservative Judaism, Philadelphia, 2001.

First Fruits of Zion, *Torah Club*, Volume 4.

Green, Arthur, *The Language of Truth, the Torah Commentary of the Sefat Emet,* The Jewish Publication Society, Philadelphia, 1998.

Hertz, Rabbi Dr. J.H., *The Pentateuch and Haftorahs*, Second Edition, Soncino Press, London, NY, 1993.

Heschel, Abraham Joshua, *I Asked for Wonder*, *A Spiritual Anthology,* The Crossroad Publishing Co., NY, 1998.

_______, *The Sabbath,* The Noonday Press, Farrar, Straus and Giroux, NY, 1996.

Hirsch, Rabbi Samson Raphael, *The Pentateuch*, Feldheim Publishers, Jerusalem / NY.

_______, *The Psalms*, Feldheim Publishers, Jerusalem / NY, 1997.

Liebowitz, Nehamah, *Studies in Bereshit /Genesis*, World Zionist Organization, Jerusalem, Israel.

______, *Studies in Bamidbar / Numbers*, World Zionist Organization, Jerusalem, Israel.

Riskin, Rabbi Shlomo, *Torah Lights, Genesis Confronts Life, Love and Family*, Ohr Torah Stone, Urim Publications, Israel, Lambda Publishers, Inc. NY, 2005.

Scheinbaum, Rabbi A.l., *Peninim on the Torah*, Noble Book Press Corp., 2000.

Zornberg, Avivah Gottlieb, *The Beginnings of Desire, Reflections on Genesis*, Image Books, Doubleday, NY, 1996.

______, *The Particulars of Rapture*, Image Books, Doubleday, NY, 2001.